Himalayan Mysticism

In all of us is hidden, the longing for the Beloved. Some people hear the calling of the heart and some others do not. As this calling starts your sacred journey, this compilation of sixty articles will explore the relationship between the Consiousness, the world-process and the soul. It will take you to experience deeper realms and layers of consciousness.

Himalayan Mysticism

Shiva's Disc To Cut Asunder And Open The Mystic Heart

RALPH NATARAJ

New Age Books

ISBN: 81-7822-289-2 (HB)
ISBN: 81-7822-290-6 (PC)

First Indian Edition: Delhi, 2006
Reprinted from Himalayan Mysticism
Shiva's disc to cut asunder and open the mystic heart.
First Published by Metavision Publishing, Netherlands.

Published by
NEW AGE BOOKS
A-44 Naraina Industrial Area, Phase-I
New Delhi-110 028 (INDIA)
Email: nab@vsnl.in
Website: www.newagebooksindia.com

For Sale in South East Asia Only

Printed in India
Nice Printing Press
3, Rashid Market Extension, New Delhi-110 051

Introduction

Do not consider what you currently carry in your hands as 'a book'. It is the gift of Shiva's disc that has the power to cut away ignorance. It contains not at all ideas to staple, that would increase the burden, as grace never works that way.These are scrolls of tantric mysticism in a contemporary language. The careful study of this work will most certainly lead to an enormous expansion of consciousness and an inner explosion of freedom. The author works hard to increase resistance in the reader and then frequently and surprisingly offers an enormous relaxation and liberating *letting go*. It is at these moments when 'the real work' is being done, similar as to how Michelangelo sculpted the David.

The book consists of 60 articles based on satsangs and explorations that Ralph Nataraj gave to his international students in 2001 and 2002. They are explorations into the curious relationship between consciousness, the world-process (Goddess Shakti) and the soul. Ralph is establishing validity for the experience of divine madness and invites the apt reader to experience deeper realms and layers of consciousness. His lucid way of writing is more like a trip with a roller coaster than listening to a mad philosopher. All the while the scrolls in this book are saturated with a mystic energy, which seems to have the uncanny power to awaken kundalini. Only the velocity of the disc is determined by the reader.

Ralph is a tantric monk. He resides in the Netherlands.

Contents

Preface

The book that you are now holding in your hands is not just another philosophical treatise about tantric mysticism. Many people had exceptional strong recognitions when they encountered these writings, while they were sent as satsangs, via the internet all around the world during the years 2001-2002. I myself experienced tremendous revelations through the work of Ralph and being in his presence. It will be interesting for you to go deeply into these texts and discover the effect it has on you. Each chapter should not be considered to be a mere chapter to be studied with the intellect, but as a precious scroll, studied with great and deep love and wonder. They contain lots of Shakti-energy. Some may make you dizzy. Some may propel you into a dazzling journey and unexpected dreams. When there is resistance as well, that is OK and in fact expected. It serves a purpose. The more tension is built up, the deeper the letting go, the liberation can be.

In this book many topics that carry a certain load for people are addressed. Ralph is trying to shake us up and get us to look from every perceivable angle to these issues; to increase the flexibility, not only of our mind, but also of our perceptions and will. For this to happen it is of great help to perform a simple consecration, to open your mind, before you start to read. This will give you the possibility to also read 'in-between the lines' where the most important information is stored.

This work is written according to the contemporary path of Yoga, Beauty & Delight of which Ralph is the preceptor. He often draws upon the tradition of Vamacari Tantra and non-dual Kashmir Saivism. Non-dual Kashmir Saivism is the philosophy of Grace and in that regard the energy that you now hold can liberate. You will get acquainted with Aghora and Sri Vidya. This book is a work in the yogic tradition, a tool on the path of courage, the path of wisdom and the path of love and an introduction into the mystery school of the Goddess.

Ralph embraces fully the dazzling paradox and leads us to the full experience of divine madness. The receptivity and awareness, with which you go through this text, is the key to make you recognise and celebrate your inherent greatness. The writer wants to offer us a good drink and I sincerely hope that you will accept joyfully and fall in love as madly as I have.

Sikandardas

'This' Side and the 'Other' Side

Many people try to understand mysticism with the mind, but that is simply impossible. Of course you want to know and to understand, but the mind can only grasp some fragmented knowledge. It can only hold some ideas and concepts, and never hold the total picture. It is not capable of real knowing. This is the difficulty in spirituality for a strong Western mind. We want to have a good family life, we want to be happy, we strive to become more successful and wealthy, and we also would like to have some 'spirituality'.

There is, however, not *some* spirituality. There is only delusion for those who are looking for that! With a strong sense of holding on and of mental supremacy, it is utterly impossible to experience real spirituality. We need to humble ourselves and lose our sense of superiority. We need to learn to bow down and admit that we don't know that much. Otherwise we would feel true peace of mind, we would have flourishing relationships and we would be totally fulfilled with the simple things that we already have. There would be no need for more. We would easily be able to share, and joyfully do so. It is the ego that never has enough and always wants more. Who pushes us forward on the ocean of desire? Never coming to rest. Never abiding in our true Self... Afraid of losing something? Afraid of drowning!

What we are looking for, we are searching for on this side. 'This side' is the earthly domain. The domain of the mind, body, senses and the elements. What we are looking for will however not be found – THERE. Anyone who is capable of some logical thinking and deduction can realize that. You need to move over HERE!

As soon as you love somebody, the seed of hate is planted and it will sprout someday. That is the realm of duality. We are looking for happiness, but because of the laws that govern this place (this side, earth, the mind-realm), it is simply impossible. We can have some momentary experiences of happiness. We can feel comfortable amidst our luxury. But we are not even really comfortable with ourselves. Our mind is always active and pushing us forward. The mind does not know rest. Always thinking. Dwelling in the past (memories) and future (expectations, desires). One thing slips away all the time and that is the present. The beautiful opening to the mystic Unknown. The eternal and infinite dimension of HERE.

There is, however, a boat awaiting you. This boat has been with you all the time. You never saw it before. You never paid attention. You had no desire to go to the other side. You wanted to go to Tenerife, France, Peru, the US, Nepal and many places, but you never had the will to really and deeply explore the inner dimension of Life. You do have an inner life. This inner life is the greatest journey or exploration. It is the real thrill. So adventurous. It is totally unmapped territory. Dragons and villains are hiding. Dark caves. Steep cliffs. Waterfalls. Tigers. The greatest treasure is not so easily available to everybody.

There is, however, a boatman who can take you across. He is a strange man. He doesn't talk much. He hides in the dark. He is not particularly looking for customers. If you ask him kindly, he might.... might be willing to take you ... Take you to the other side. **HERE.**

The other side is Heaven. This is not after death. It is not even an out-of-body-experience. It is a total in-body experience. 'The other side' is the experiencing of Oneness. It is the mystical realm. The other dimension of life (or is it the only dimension?). Experiencing It is awakening. Jesus said that the Kingdom of Heaven is within. It is available for everybody. It is the Garden where we roam around in ecstasy, hearing divine music, smelling intoxicating flowers. It is the domain of love, peace and bliss. The other side is everywhere. Once you are on the other side, there is no more 'this side' and 'the other side'. They merge. The border between the earth and the sky disappears. All 'Theres' are Here. You see your Beloved everywhere. This is the supreme Abode, the only thing worth attaining, although It cannot be 'attained'. You are no longer bothered by *thine* and *mine*. That is only mind-stuff on the other side (the other other side) and has nothing to do with the Free Dome (real freedom).

It is always there (Here) and not far away at all. It was never born and will never die. It cannot be compartmentalized. No one has the privilege. It has no divisions like penthouse suites. Only one person is not welcome to this magnificent place and that is your mind. You will have to leave it behind. It is not capable of enjoying such a heavenly abode. That is why it must die and you need a second birth. But don't be afraid. We tantriks are very loving people. We like to go back and forth, in and out, up and down. We love the matrix. Not being stuck in any one 'place'. We like to experience all dimensions of life. To pierce each dimension. To travel deep and far into the Unknown. And to accept that we cannot and do not need to know 'everything'.

Before you are ready for the GREAT boat trip, you need to become friends with yourself and be a LOVER OF LIFE. We are not talking about a cerebral experience at all. This is the ultimate experience for any true lover. You need to be a gypsy, a bohemian. Have you experienced the delight of being with your lover and the pain of being separated from Him or Her? Or were you so afraid of the pain that you could never be hurt? Because, then my friend, it is better that you first roam around some more. Start to live and open your eyes. This precious book is not for those who are counting their money. Are you ready to embrace the flowers that your lover gives you even when you know that a dagger is hidden amidst the soft and sweet smelling petals?

Soul Searching

In all of us is hidden the longing for the Beloved. Some people hear the Calling of the heart and others do not (yet). This Calling starts our sacred journey. It is a mysterious one...

We talk about God and have our ideas and concepts of God. This is, however, not God. It is our ideas and concepts of what God is, but please understand that that is not God. God either reveals Him- or Herself to you or not. In the beginning, there are some glimpses. In the Sivastotravali, Utpaladeva describes this very beautifully, and the yearning that it gives rise to. It is this yearning for the Beloved that is so sacred in Sufism.

There are two things at work: we need to do self-inquiry and come to know the mind and the ego. The more the mind thins out and loses its grip, the stronger the Self shines through. We have to do our part, which is strong spiritual practice. Some people think that pursuit of pleasure leads automatically to liberation. That is certainly not so. The ocean of repetitive history is endless.

The tantrik walks a very narrow path. On one side is the abyss of arrogance leading to narcissism, and on the other side a fake humbleness, which is nothing else but an expression of low self-esteem. If you suffer from low self-esteem there is not much for you to find here. Arrogance will be slain down and narcissists will be keelhauled. We need some common sense and I challenge you to develop your intellect to full fruition. It is only with a sharp and awakened buddhi (higher intellect) that we can slay the monster of ignorance upon which Lord Nataraja dances His cosmic dance.

The Self is not to be found or searched for. It is and was always here. We can only allow our ego to be broken down by a skilled hammerer. And support his work by being responsible and doing self-inquiry. We need to step out of the way. That is in fact the only thing.

We are not out to improve the personality. Of what use is that? Most people pick up pebbles while there are diamonds right in front of them. I am talking about an infinite treasure and most people desire a good beach. If you try to follow me with your mind, you will fail, as that is a sheer impossibility. Shiva churns the ocean but your mouth is too tiny to encompass the truth. Only the heart truly knows. But please remember that I am not talking about silly new age ideas. The Heart is triadic!

When the personality has many wounds, it is important to work through these and to purify the heart. With low self-esteem it is hard for God's Grace to reach us. Tantra is for the vira (hero). This means that there has to be some-one. There needs to be a personality. A strong one who finally comes to realize that in order to know God we have to go beyond the personality. The personality cannot know God. Something very finite cannot know the infinite, which was always there. We have to leave the known behind and at least stick our toe into feeling the temperature of the divine paradox.

One of the biggest secrets in life is that God hid Herself in the creation. God is not to be found out-side. Most of us have ambitions in the earthly realm. Yet the Kingdom of God is within. In order to be successful in the earthly realm, we work with greed, lust, ambition, desire, manipulation, lies etc. It is the domain of the ego. Walking in the Garden fills us up with love, peace and freedom. This same love, peace and freedom cannot be found in the realm of the world. Oh yes, we need to live in the world all right. I am talking about full realization in the body and about living in the world. I am not talking about a heavenly abode somewhere else. That is the domain of religions and I am not religious in that sense. They try to sell you some heaven and use 'hell' as a scarecrow. JC already indicated fairly accurately how to get there, and that you do not need a church nor a priest, so why did they build these huge buildings, become the biggest owner of real estate worldwide and invent a hierarchy of impostors (popes, cardinals, priests etc.) who supposedly can show us the door?

The door is not far away. Whenever you are offered a choice, you take another door. That is up to you. But you don't even have to leave your house in order to find the Kingdom. In fact you don't even have to wink. You don't need to pay anyone money. God doesn't care more about righteous (or moralistic) people than sinners, although I have a feeling that gypsies and lovers – those who are in ecstasy – dance through the Portes du Soleil without even knowing it. Suddenly they find themselves in heaven. The sacred dance of Nataraj is unfolding right in front of their eyes. Aim for ecstasy amidst Divine Madness. Ecstasy is not to be found by party-people. Joy is quite something else. Ecstasy comes upon losing the mind. It happens unexpectedly. You cannot set out to do it, as then the mind will be very alert and defend its foothold.

It is a lifestyle. You have been focused outward for a long, long time. Some readers finally understand something about the inner journey. The shadow. Demons. Mythical figures. Fairy tales. They are not there for nothing. They are all signposts along the trail. Many tests for you to pass. You need courage. It is not the work of one night. Better to schedule many years, my friend. You may need decades or lifetimes to arrive at that very instant called the everything and everywhere.

But this truly is the most precious thing for a man or woman. It is the only worthwhile objective. The only valuable experience. If you were only to know how precious it is to have a human body... The capabilities are enormous. You are not a man but a God-man. God is taking birth in or through you. But this 'you' must die. Most people are not ready for that. So there are long spiritual practices to prepare you for the shock.

Can you make a picture of God and focus on her attributes? Which attributes do you imagine God to have? Please write down some.

....

Now zoom in on these attributes and manifest and live them in your life. God reveals herself to you in the intensity that you can handle. Become more like God. Live as a proud human being, while at the same time it is important to be humble. Develop a relationship as a servant to God. Even the very wise ones – upon full God-realisation – regard themselves as a servant to Her. A very bold one has the relationship of a spouse (lover). The Dervish trembles! You are however the king, the queen and the tiger.

We don't have to give up who we are but our 'sense' of who we are. We are hugely deluded. This is indescribable. That is why I suggest folks study the movie 'The Matrix'. It makes it very clear.

The qualifications of a good student on the spiritual path are severe. They almost make up a master. The disciple needs to prepare himself to confront (come vis-à-vis with) the boatman. A student has a relationship with his mind. Those relationships are not worthwhile and interesting on the Path of Yoga, Beauty & Delight. This is the path of the heart.

You need to make a strong effort to make your body strong, to refine your senses and antennae, to dilute the footholds of the mind, to develop will-power and discipline, to develop a noble character, to develop compassion for all living beings and to open your heart. How to open the heart?

Allow it to be hurt. Offer it to be crushed. Walk with open eyes into the dagger that your friend carries.

Feel love for everybody – especially for those who are obnoxious, obstinate and very difficult to love. Make room for all of them in your heart. And then feel compassion for all those souls who are suffering. And I am not only talking of Palestinians and poor children in Africa. Many people are suffering. Suffering is 3-fold and until (every) one is fully realised, there is suffering.

What are your thirst and your longing aimed at?

The spiritual journey is very difficult. There are only a few authentic paths that can take you to the end and across. Many are endless loops. All these experiences are worthwhile. A master in the esoteric order of the Holy Fire has tremendous powers to liberate someone. The tradition of Shaktipata – one of the biggest secrets in esoteric schools – is developed to the fullest in Kashmir Sorcery.

We have many ideas about spirituality. It has to permeate our entire life. We cannot be spiritual for two weeks a year or one hour a day and for the rest, just carry on with our ego. You have to cut down to the very essence.

This is not a simple job my friends, and you need to come well prepared. I am saying that only one desire must remain. Your will has to be sharpened to only one will and that is the Will of the Almighty. That is how you must humble yourself.

If you have a job, a family and other responsibilities, you need to take care of all those. I am not saying that you should become a monk. I am saying that you have to do some work.

You must be aware of every time that you fall out of multi-dimensional awareness and how, where and why.

You identify with an 'I'. But this 'I' is a false identification. You need to experience this for yourself. That means you have to do self-inquiry. Slowly but steadily in the spiritual process, you come to know yourself as a totally different I. An I that encompasses and embraces everybody. An I that is filled with bliss, peace, love and compassion. An I that encompasses the whole universe. Because enlightenment is not an individual effort. What use is it that you are 'enlightened' while everybody around you is suffering? Live for others. Those who only live for themselves are more dead than alive.

Let's all come alive and let there be a Sangha (spiritual family).

Shaktipata

Now I will share with you the highly esoteric secret of Shaktipata.

The Shakti of Shiva!

Read well, my friend, and understand. There is only one supreme Being, one supreme Reality, that which we call Paramashiva, God. Absolute consciousness beyond birth. Unfathomable. Beyond language. Totally incomprehensible for any mind. It is something that must be experienced! But how? How does this work?

It is part of the divine play, the Lila. It is the sport of Shiva. It is the nature of Shiva as consciousness, to manifest. To sprout. This is totally a matter of his free will (Svatantrya). It is not like a seed that only sprouts if the conditions (sun, water, season, fertility of the ground) are right.

In this divine consciousness is a slight stirring. A divine throb. This is the 'principle' of Spanda. Spanda, like Shaktipata, is unique to non-dual Kashmir Saivism. The Spanda happens in Shakti. God is not transformed in any way. He is not 'changed' in any way, nor is He in any way 'affected' by His creation. Pure, undifferentiated consciousness is pure, undifferentiated consciousness = Shiva. In Shakti, Iccha, Jnana and Kriya arise. The creation happens out of bliss. It is a blissful cosmic surge. Like an orgasm, but then much, much more, because it is cosmic and not only in the gross realm of a body that is ruled by a mind in ignorance. How does the ignorance of the mind arise? Listen carefully. Concentrate.

Most religions and philosophies explain that ignorance is without a beginning. According to non-dual Kashmir Saivism this is not correct. The world has a beginning although nobody can trace it back to an exact 'date'. Everything in the world has a beginning and an end, but not Supreme Existence or Paramashiva. Paramashiva is without a beginning and without an end. It always was, is and will be. It is timeless and space-less. It is the creator of time and space. Listen carefully and let us try to understand precisely how 'time' and 'space' were created.

They are sheaths, covers. They hold the 'ignorance'. The matrix and the mind are both a sheath and a contraction of Shiva. They exist in Shiva as consciousness. Not as matter, but as an appearance. Like a dream. Not like an illusion. It is a delusion. Come to understand.

Pierce!

Use your faculties well!

It is for a reason that you are now holding this book.

Shiva has five powers: Projection, Preservation, Absorption, Concealment (Obscuration) and Revelation! This Revelation is the Shaktipata, Grace.

When Shiva reveals Himself as the universe, He hides his essence of consciousness. This is the concealment. This is the world that you see when you look out of the window. The world that has been pulled over your eyes (Morpheus). This is when ignorance started, although it is not traceable to a certain date. The mind can not grasp this.

When the spiritual journey starts for a man this is, in fact, due to divine Grace or the fifth power of Shiva, called Revelation. The revelation works for a human being as Shaktipata. It is the ascent. God first descends as concealment, as creation. The whole diverse psychic apparatus is created. The entire matrix arises with the mind(s). Huge confusion. A magical and unbelievable show of the diversity through the duality of the mind.

In the same way that mankind has nothing to do with the show of concealment of Shiva, the spiritual ascent only starts when Shiva activates His fifth power of Anugraha.

Even the Upanishads write about Shaktipata, but they emphasise what man can do, such as meditation, contemplation, living purely, being vegetarian, practising Hatha Yoga, Karma Yoga, Bhakti Yoga, Jnana Yoga, Raja Yoga etc. It is only Kashmir Saivism that thoroughly explains the working of Shaktipata. It is the essence of this philosophy. Shaktipata is the essence of the guru. That is why the guru has such an important place and position in non-dual Kashmir Saivism. He enlivens the life-force of Kundalini.

Lord Shiva in the form of the guru comes to the rescue of his loyal devotees. The start of the spiritual journey for a man is really the bestowal of light Shaktipata. There are 9 categories of Shaktipata. In fact there are 36. Devotion arises in the heart of the disciple as the result of the rise of Shakti, Kundalini. When the devotion and the sadhana become stronger, the Lord is almost obliged to increase the Shaktipata. With stronger Shaktipata or with stronger Shakti-energy rising as the snake Kundalini in our spine, the devotion becomes stronger automatically. Some of you must have felt this strong devotion at times. It is a divine love affair. That is the destiny of this ship! That is what we are sailing towards. We are heading for a beautiful island.

It is a love affair between the small self and the big Self.

Between the disciple and the master.

Between man and God.

Shakti and Shiva.

This is the essence of Tantra.

Listen carefully .... Let's go deeper.

With the Shaktipata the devotion arises. The spiritual journey starts and you come to doubt or question the matrix. You begin to search your mind. You look for help. You start some spiritual practice. That is the activation of Divine Grace! It is the power of consciousness working through you!

The light begins to shine. A small candle is lit. It is its destiny to emerge and to become a mighty fire. Either this life or another! Once Shaktipata rises, it continues to rise in a next life. Non-dual Kashmir Saivism is so mysterious in its essence – these gurus and masters are so incredibly strong, determined and powerful; their love for you, me and us is so strong – that they promise to continue to work with you in your next life. You don't know yet exactly what we are talking about here, like Neo before he got unplugged. He only sensed that something was wrong. Right understanding came MUCH later. This revelation is bound for the entire ocean of Paramashiva.

People view Shaktipata in different ways. Some think that human beings can force Shaktipata to rise by an incredibly strong sadhana, meaning that only one desire remains. When all of life is committed to one aim, it is bound to happen. Others assert that Shaktipata operates totally separate from the small will of human beings. That it has nothing to do with that. According to others it operates by chance. Some explain this chance as two co-existing energies working together. The energies are opposite and a result of two equally strong karmas (one 'negative' so to say and 'one' positive) of the past.

Shaktipata is a great mystery. The Shakti is available for everybody. It resides in all of us at the base of our spine. Some hold that through tantric practice, this Kundalini energy will rise. That we can make it rise. *That* also is a false notion and exemplifies incorrect understanding. Some say that the Grace continually pours down on us.

Of the five powers of Shiva, 'obscuration' comes after projection, preservation and absorption, and before revelation. The obscuration happens with the six sheaths; the tattvas of limited capacity to do, limited capacity to know, narrowing of the scope of our attention interest; introduction of causality and sequence, sense of time (we were, are and shall be) plus the great principle of obscuration: the MAYA!
Ignorance basically arose with the 'creation' of the six sheaths! Of course our minds called it so. In Shiva there is no language. Only the mind utilises language. The mind exists because of words. This is explained precisely in Kashmir Saivism in the theory of Paravak.

'Our' psychic apparatus is buddhi (higher mind / pure intellect), manas (the mind) and ahamkara (ego). The rise of Shakti illumines us from within. Before, we were always outwardly directed. With the spiritual journey we turn our attention within. Shiva and Shakti are the subtlest of the subtle. The most sublime of the most sublime. We work into more subtle realms. We develop our inner senses and later on we move beyond even them.

Supreme Reality cannot be grasped by the mind. The mind is never able to experience something as profound, huge, mysterious, vast, deep, and paradoxical as the supreme Reality, which is One. Only Shiva is the real observer, just as Shakti is the only 'experiencer'. You must lose your mind and then Reality experiences Reality in or 'through' your nervous system and that is what you are made for. To be enlightened in the flesh. While you have a body. This is the glorious opportunity that you have. It is a great gift. Highly auspicious. Even the celestial beings have a beginning and are thus not the Supreme Reality Itself, which is without beginning and without an end.

Human Beings are the most highly evolved species on earth. Of course there are other species and celestial beings (even super celestial Beings) in this universe. We are about to meet them. When we do some fierce sadhana and work on ourselves. We have to cleanse and purify our hearts. Let's not waste our time. Realise the great opportunity at hand. Dive into your own Being. Develop will power and have strong devotion. Love all mankind. Every single one. Every living human being.

Through the Lila of Shiva, the obscuration marks the beginning of the basic ignorance of the individual person in whose form He starts to appear. Realise your divine Nature. What you see around you with your outer senses is the evolution of ignorance (maya). It is the amazing psychic diversity that we encounter in this world. The world is as we see it.

The ascent of Shiva is the so-called second part of the drama of Shiva whereby He re-appears again (Revelation). It is the 36 tattvas back (up). Because of this Revelation (Shaktipata,

Grace), the human being realises his oneness with God. He sees and experiences everything as the expression of himself. He realises the workings – the web – of the matrix. Tantra also means to weave. We unravel the net that got stuck. We take the knots out. Maybe it is better to say that we allow the knots to be taken out. We give permission, although consciousness is certainly not dependent on our permission at any time.

We have to become empty. We have to merge. We need to surrender. It cannot be done by the mind. We have to be unplugged. Only Morpheus and his crew can do that. The human being can do strong sadhana and spiritual practice, but there are no guarantees. It is all up to the Revelation and Grace of Shiva. This grace manifests as strong self-effort. It is all according to His divine will. Only a tantrik (mystic) has the power to intervene. An enlightened person is not a person anymore. Some people say that it is even more fortunate to be a realised human being than to be an angel or Shiva Himself. Because this is the Self-referral process. The Self experiencing It-Self.

Seek these people. They can guide you. Treat them with reverence. The Sadguru comes to the rescue of his most loyal devotees. He reminds you of your essence. But he is (mysteriously and seemingly) bound by certain rules. The Shaktipata he transmits has to be equal to the devotion and certain conditions in the disciple. A disciple must qualify himself. The guru transmits any form of mild or strong Shaktipata only to certain qualified disciples.

So do your sadhana! Grow stronger in will and devotion!

The Antenna

This internet seems to be a vast place and my computer is an antenna. We can both point our antenna to receive the same channel.

Who is broadcasting on that channel?

Your body is like an antenna.

An antenna in an ocean of frequencies.

Would you prefer to see Discovery, MTV, CNN or Nederland 1?

Do you know that you have sensors in your hand? When you practise Tai Chi-like movements (slowly), you will feel that there is a difference in temperature in your hands with the in-breath and the out-breath.

They say that our eighth chakra is in our feet. There is some truth in this, although 'officially' Tantra explains about six chakras only. Most people think that there are seven, but the Sahasrara (7th) is not considered to be a chakra. It is more of a 'space'. Some people localise this space above the crown of our head. It is thus not in the skull, but slightly above the body.

We have to get used to understanding that we are not only the physical body. You are more than your skin, memories, digestion, name, thoughts, conditionings, habits, feelings and reactions. The body is an intricate flow of energy. That is the truth in the 'middle' realm. The flow of energy through the nadis. There are supposedly 72.000 of these nadis, although some books explain that there are 72.000.000 of them. The spiritual path is one of purification, refinement, realisation and ascension.

The way our chakras are tuned, steers the flow of this energy. This influences how we feel, what we know and what we can remember. Our remembering can go very deep. Much more than the memories of this lifetime, into the realm of 'knowing' and the akashic-records (celestial memory-bank)

This remembering does not come via study, intellectual analysis, reading or discussions. That is, however, the only thing that the western mind is familiar with and has faith and confidence in. There is so much more. For that we need to let go. All letting go is of the mind. Morpheus explains to NEO why he can't unplug that many people: 'The mind has trouble letting go!'

So, there is the physical body that we know well and strongly identify with for good reasons. In this body we feel emotions. That is a different circuit from the physical body. They are however intertwined. That is why emotions release through deep tissue massage and other forms of bodywork.

We have to work through the body and through these emotions to discover a hidden realm. Working through the body and emotions also means letting go of repressed memories. It means recycling a part of our 'karma'. We go deeper within and (re)discover the inner realm. More and more awareness comes to the front. We hit deeper dimensions. Some release of stress is bound to happen. This happens in all sorts of ways: laughing, bodily pain or discomfort, jerks, insomnia, illness, 'new age spiritual experiences' etc.

At a certain point we experience more peace, bliss, love, balance, stillness, connectedness and wisdom. Our self-knowledge becomes strong and clear. Upon deeper inquiry we scratch deeper levels of being and start with the inner travels through vast realms. New dimensions are discovered. We start to see the mind for what it is: a useful tool. But you are becoming less and less a slave. More mastery arises.

Knowledge and experience need to go hand in hand. Most Westerners read many books. We would be in favour of reading much less and doing more spiritual practice. Under the guidance of a master would be best. He or she can give individual assignments and help you to break out of the mind by breaking your conditioning and challenging all your (false) thought-concepts and ideas. He kindles a flame in your heart. He helps you to let go (of falsity) and to remember.

By this you can actually meditate. You start to know what real meditation is. This means a quantum leap forward in your spiritual progress.
From the deepest viewpoint in Kashmir Saivism, all that I said before is false. There is only a stir in consciousness. There is no reincarnation and no karma. 'Spiritual progress' is knowledge and knowledge is bondage. We can travel beyond the realm of cause and effect, back through time, through the wall of space, leaving behind our false concepts of limited knowing, limited creativity and limited being. We are allowed a glimpse of the divine and recognise it as our true nature. Imagined boundaries vanish. No more curtains veil us. The merging in lovemaking of Shiva and Shakti. They unite in bliss. Unending creativity. Infinitely deep 'dreams' in meditation. Whole universes arise, expand and contract outside of the realm of time. It happens in an instant. It lasts eternally.

You can feel these waves in your body, which is an antenna. Draw your attention within. Many practices in Kashmir Saivism entail drawing your attention in and 'looking back' to the height of certain intense moments in the external world. Like the moment of a sudden breakthrough. Or suddenly seeing the misery on the battlefield. A totally unexpected meeting with an old friend. At the height of intense pleasure. Amidst overwhelming beauty. During a wild dance. At the moment of sudden life-threatening danger. These are great moments to realise. Looking at a deep abyss. Recognising. That is the mystical experience in Kashmir Saivism. It stands in the middle of life. In Kashmir Saivism it is perfect to have a house, a family and a job. There are many opportunities to practise yoga. Yoga even in the midst of bhoga (enjoying).

This is very different to renouncing. Some people do not understand the practices of Kashmir Saivism. It is often thought that we have to renounce pleasure. What a strange way of thinking and reasoning ... What is wrong with pleasure? Is beauty to be avoided? NO! That is the way for the 'weak'. An animal in the jungle lives in tune with his surroundings and is aware. The same is possible for us. The stones are not there accidentally. The flowers are there for a reason. This world is beautiful. There is an exchange between me and the trees. The seasons affect my body. My endocrine system is different at new moon to at full moon. Do you think that the stars are just there to serve as decoration for human beings on planet earth?

You need to develop and use your subtle systems of perception and knowing. Travel in new spheres. Stretch yourself out beyond the boundaries of skin and skull. What is the difference between the stars and you? What do you have in common?

Where is your base?

What is 'life'?

What can you not see and hear (yet)?

Sense the antennae in your feet at this moment. Close your eyes and feel right now how strong these sensors are in fact!

....

Tune in to your body. Notice where you feel.

Notice where you know.

Notice the space around you.

The space in-between thoughts.

The space that is everywhere.

If you become really quiet and still, what happens? What do you sense?

What do you know?

Use your antennae!

It is a Blue Connection

We all like to study creation. But how about 'maintenance' (preservation) and 'dissolution' (absorption)?

Dissolution is a better word than *destruction*. Shiva destroys ignorance but not 'the universe'. The universe He dissolves. He takes it back within. It is in fact an absorption. How does this work?

Brahma, Vishnu, Maheshvara

These are considered to be the triple powers.

It is one thing to create the universe, but a second thing to maintain (preserve) it. It is an easy thing to fall in love, but quite a lot of work to maintain a 30-year old relationship.

It is one thing to create a fire. It is another thing to keep it burning.

It is one thing to have a nice experience during meditation, but how to allow it to permeate our entire life?

Right now this book is upheld by power, although it seemingly does (not) exist. Even matter is just energy in motion. It all flickers in and out of existence. This one quark disappears '*here*' and reappears somewhere totally different later on. Existence is quite marvellous.

This page is white but what are white holes? It is not unimportant to understand.

A black hole absorbs all matter and energy. They simply disappear in it. Whole solar systems and galaxies. It is not that the energy is *transformed* or *stored*. Stephen Hawking describes very accurately in 'A brief history of time' what would happen if you saw a clock falling into a black hole.

You see, this way, all of the universe can be dissolved into nothing.

That is the third power of Shiva.

It depends on whether he is in deep meditation or whether Shakti is able to get His attention with her intoxicating dance.

This, my friends, is the blue connection. It is a connection IN and **with** and out of, but especially **IN** LOVE.

Praise him who hides HimSelf so well:
The lover of lovers
The Master of Masters
The *greatest* of all 'magicians'
The adorable One
The creator of wonderland
The designer of *The Matrix*
The supreme lover
The eternal dweller
The bearer of the skull
The ascetic and the cosmic dancer
Destroyer of ignorance
Please set your eye on me and finish me
I long to drink your nectar
Oh churner of the ocean of divine ambrosia
Pour me another drink
Let me become drunk with your love
I long to stumble through the doorway...
Intoxicated...
So that I see your garden with one eye
My ears hear only one melody
I cannot remain standing anymore
I must dance
My lungs scream out:

Om Namah Shivaya

Where do you hide?
In the heart of the Beloved?
But you are my Beloved...
I long to know her, by which – loving her – I adore and love everybody
So that only the dance of love remains
That ferocious dance by which ignorance is destroyed
Please aim your arrow and let it squash right through my heart
I wish to share my joy, love and happiness with everybody

Don't want to keep it inside anymore
My heart bursts open
With the *thought* of you
One thought and I already die
Let me drown in your ocean
I indeed see the Beloved everywhere
Why was she hiding for so long?
Or was I too busy?
I wonder...
I wander...
Always in search of you
I worship every flower
In the hope of finding you there
After dancing all night
I fall on the floor
And there I discovered you again
Oh you...
So mysterious in your plays
You keep me an alert fool.

Tantric 'Lovemaking'

Tantra – especially in the West – is shrouded in misconceptions and confusions.

It is not very useful to learn how to pump the air into the left rear tyre of the car. We need a lot more than only air in that tyre. We have to be able to put the tyres on and take them off. The car is intricate machinery that works together. Tyres differ in size, shape and quality. The Concorde has new tyres that I believe cost many millions per tyre. It is very important that the pressure in the tyre is at the right level. However, we also need to learn the workings of the car. How to steer, how to use the gears, how to fix this and that. What rules to obey in traffic? How to drive on a soaking wet road? How to steer during a skid?

Lovemaking is a beautiful thing. Tantra has very little to do with that.

A tantric student usually lives a celibate life for a long time. Tantra is only for the vira! It is not a thing that we in the West can adopt to make our life more comfortable and *interesting*... We are talking about a very ancient and authentic philosophy. Tantra existed thousands of years before Jesus Christ. The lineage is unbroken and the transfer is very precise.

However, we are not only learning how to drive a car, but learning to fly a modern aeroplane: concentrated, relaxed and present. A plane that can land on water, stall in mid-air, land on a ship or on an island. A plane that can go backwards in space and forwards in time. A plane that can suddenly 'disappear' and that can become so small that it can enter our veins.

The master will guide you in the practice. Nothing is shared about the practice. It is highly individual. Disciples are not supposed to talk about their individual practice with others. The practice is highly secretive because it is individualised. What one person is doing might not be beneficial at all for another. It is an unfortunate thing that some things have leaked out and are now (mis)used by people who really know very little about authentic Tantra. Original Tantra should only be practised under the guidance and in the energy of your master.

You should do all that you can to prepare by yourself. It might go very well. The master may appear to you in your dreams. It is possible to receive initiations that way. It has happened before.

Be very careful when you ask to be accepted as a disciple. Know very well who you are going to ask. Choosing a guru is as auspicious as selecting your spouse. You can always separate from your spouse and take another one. Your master may be with you for several lifetimes. You can visit many gurus. And in fact you should. Check them out. See what works for you and what does not. Don't particularly look for *a charismatic person*. There are many *frauds*. Make sure you get to know someone thoroughly before requesting to be accepted as a disciple. Once he or she accepts you as a disciple, a very peculiar *relationship* starts to unfold. The guru will shake you. That is his job!

The greatest magician

Who wants this Divine Madness anyway?

Why should we thirst for that?

Isn't it perhaps better to be liberated?

To be like the pope?

Or like an ascetic? Like Buddha?

What is so great about Divine Madness?

Maybe I should desire to go to another one...?

Divine Madness is not for everyone!

You must be a bit crazy.

But no more than an alert fool.

To recognize the senses as the deluders that they are.

Cooperating with the biggest magician on earth:

....

The MIND...

Well, he's not the biggest. Just the biggest on earth. Earth is a tiny place, friends. It is merely a speck of dust. Saivists always realized that. They have knowing. They don't need to practise science and read books. They know in their consciousness, just as 'Knowledge is structured in consciousness!' I was taught to severely examine this when I was 12 years old. To understand the depth of that sentence is not easy.

Today, most people behave and walk around like sheep. They believe most things they are told. No effort at sincere self-inquiry. No strong wish to really know. What is real?

That takes a hero. In Tantra and Sanskrit, they call it vira, which is usually translated as 'hero', but actually means a noble person. A civilized one. Tantra is not for curious folk who are happy with their pathetic lives. There must be a strong longing in your heart. We call it 'The Calling'. We need the hero to examine the shadow that he is. We have to build up the discipline to finally – after many years of struggling – fall prey and surrender to that beautiful dancing girl who soothes our forehead and balms our hands that have fought so fiercely.

We need the strength to look the knowledge that we have gathered and gained, right in the eye and see it for the thief and criminal that it is: a huge and nasty monster.

We do not need to be modest. We need the arrogance to realize who we really are and to dare to live it. To turn into a lion. But a lion with manners. A lion that can relax and have an overview. Know that the weathers and the seasons will change and realise that the wisdom and force by which the seasons change is Herself changeless.

In the same way that above is no different from below.

The trees have mighty branches above the ground, but underneath the ground – in the realm that we cannot pierce with our physical eyes – there is the same network of roots. It is the exact mirror image. And the deeper your roots will go into the dark, the higher your branches will grow into the sky (heaven) and towards the sun. There is thesis and anti-thesis.

You need to learn to look into the dark. To confront the dark Goddess Kali. Jesus had his 40 days in the desert. Buddha his 40 days sitting against a tree. Hafiz the 40 nights in front of the statue of a saint. The dark night of the soul. You have to learn to travel through subtle realms. The mythical realm. We are in the West and things work differently here. There are no initiations in the jungle for a boy to become a man and no rituals for girls when they first menstruate. But these are all magical moments. Our life is filled with magical moments. I NOW live in a magical moment where the whole universe is conspiring.

It is when you are there that the matrix starts. Right there you can enter the rabbit hole. Platform 9 3/4 is not hard to find for those who desire – who long and thirst for – Living Water. The truth. Divine Madness. Time is the greatest magician.

Surrender is certainly not for the weak. They will only get lost. Surrender is something very difficult but inevitable in the end. Surrender is the doorway to the sun: Portes du Soleil. You need to give up that which you think you are, and this is the one thing that people do not want to let go of. They are willing to go, what they feel is, very far. For us it is laughable. You must be willing to give to the Lord all that you are, in order to become who you are. In order to realize your divine identity. This is a shock for you that you need to prepare well for. Reading poems from Hafiz and Lalleshvari will surely help.

Abstract reasoning is mostly childish. People try to catch the knowledge that they long for, not realizing that it is the monster that will slay them, just as I* am the murderer of your self, which many readers don't realize yet. You think you are going for a, hopefully, nice sailing trip. It will turn out quite differently...

Are you aware of what left-handed Tantra or Aghora really is?

Live in wonder. Do not look for certainty!

* At places like this, the author does not refer to himself, but to the magical 'I' of consciousness.

On Kali

Kali is the female form of 'Kala'. Kala means time. She is a dark Goddess. She looks terrible. She is black and is allied to the forces of death. She does not look ethical or aesthetically interesting. It takes a vira to approach Her. She is almost a curse.

She is fascinating because we have to traverse the terrible. This is the allure of Kali.

Time governs the universe. Time is, in fact, eternity. Everything changes, except the force by which everything changes, and that is eternity. It is only on this side that everything seems to be going forward. We have not yet grasped the essence and the mystery of time. There is a secret message in time itself. Very hard to find. The Mother of time is un-born, un-created and un-dying Reality beyond all cause, forms and appearances (abhasa). Time hides the Mother of time, who is eternal. Time only seemingly passes in the mirror of magic.

Time makes things grow and change. Through time human beings get to recognize the womb of time, hidden in a frozen time-space continuum like a clock. It is a huge mystery. It takes slowing down. Kali is the divine net, in which we will fall when we jump into the abyss. She spirals us into eternity and divinity. IF we approach her the right way.

The right way is of course the left way and the left way is the right way. Time is the breath of spirit. It is that matrix by which all events in the universe are perched on the skyline of space.

Time is the rhythm to which Shiva dances his Cosmic Dance. Time is the Mother who eats Her children.

Yet, in this devouring of Her children, She also returns them to wholeness, waking-up and realization. It is the true gift. The highest boon. It is the return to Yoga, Beauty & Delight. Time is birth and death. Eternity spans over both. We are this eternity, and yet we are afraid to lose time. We treasure (or hate) the past and hope for the future. Afraid to die... To die to the lie. The lie of time. Kali shocks us and wakes us to drink eternity from Her bosom. If we lose our attachment to the events in our life, we gain mastery over time itself.

Kali holds great secrets about the universe. In order to create, we first have to learn to destroy. In order to bring in the new, we must first be able to do away with the old. This applies to many levels.

Kali is the Goddess of destruction who leaves nothing behind. We have to allow all of our attachments to the material world to be destroyed. We must move beyond our ignorance and leave the mind behind. We must be willing to be and act crazy. We must offer our head to be crushed.

We need to long for the feeling of the cold double-edged sword as it glides through our neck, chopping off 'our head' (ego). We must be willing to relinquish all ideas, projections, beliefs, models and identifications. Offer all that belongs to the small individual self into the huge blazing fire of homa (spiritual fire). We must be willing to sacrifice ourselves. Only by the wise act of sacrificing our ego can we truly move beyond the bonds of ignorance. Kali is the wise matriarchal Goddess who accepts this kind of sublime offering.

Kali is our life. She is our breath and the energy that flows through our channels in the form of Shakti. It is through Her that we live. She is our very life. The essence of our vitality. It is Her magic, brilliance and sublime intelligence that makes our body perform miracles.

Kali is associated with blood. She drinks Her own blood and renews Life itself through all kinds of bodily processes. She is life, blood and breath itself. Kali is also death and thus the doorway to the eternal. Our real birth. Death is the start of the Beginning. THINGS ARE NOT WHAT THEY APPEAR TO BE! Death is the ending of that which is unreal. Because of death, that which is inessential makes way for the Essential to shine forth. The Essence is hidden in in-essence. Thus spiritual death is the gateway to the Eternal.

There is ebb and flow. The sea is continuously moving. Death comes to life and life seems to die. It is a huge mystery that we will never know unless we step through the opening. Can you be conscious of life in death and death in life? What is the reality of this? A Kali-worshipper dies daily. That is the worship. To be empty. To offer the ego into the blazing fire of consciousness. To pray to be devoured. To die even to likes and dislikes.

When we make our mind empty all the time, each moment is fresh and thus life becomes a divine meditation.

On Forms

We all remember some-where that there is in fact only consciousness. This awareness has existed all the time. It never died and was never born. It cannot be measured or divided. It has no depth, no surface, no width, no colour, no hiding place. It is not male or female. It is not air nor is it space. It isn't even 'emptiness'. It is not it. It simply IS, as you are. NO LABEL WILL DO. No word is good enough. Labels and words are always relative. A mind can therefore never understand what consciousness is, although it is consciousness. An eye cannot see itself. You can never see your entire body at once. If you look into the mirror to see your back, you cannot see the front. Even a camera with a wide-angle lens does not see the face of the viewer / filmer. Light moves through a lens or a crystal and the light is distorted, although light remains light. To know awareness means you have to be awareness.

Now that is fairly simple. This awareness reflects and it becomes consciousness so that it can become aware of itself. It does that through you.

Consciousness manifested in 'sound' and 'form'. There is a primordial sound and there is a primordial form. That is why we say that Tantra = Mantra + Yantra.

The form evolved into earth, water and sky. The earth evolved into a plant and the plant became a tree. Spiritual teachings were always delivered under a tree. And what now is this book? Is this book not a tree?

Let's try to answer this question whether or not this book is in fact the same as a tree. What do you think?

The Formless developed into man, animals and plants.

Are they different? In the very beginning man was just running around naked and eating berries and stuff. Later on he began to cover himself. Then he stored the food in a certain place and he developed a sense of 'ownership'. Who invented ownership? The mind of men. They defended 'ownership' to death, and killed for their ideas of 'ownership'. Like men of today still do. Very wise and very religious men in the name of God, Allah or whomever.

Animals and plants also have consciousness. I am sure you are aware of that. How else could you have found your way to a book like this? Yes, there is life in animals and plants. Maybe you cannot hear the plant talking, but that does not at all mean that they do not talk. This is silly science-stuff from the so-called most brilliant minds on the planet. And their conclusion is that: "if they cannot hear plants talk, they cannot talk!" What silly and childish form of intelligence is that? Who ever said that there are no other life forms in this entire galaxy? You must be pretty dogmatic to state such a thing when astronomers know that there are 12.000.000.000 suns in the Milky Way...

I am appealing to your intelligence, not to your conditioned knowledge and the boring concepts that people have tried to place in your skull. Step out of it!

You must be able to imagine that first there was maybe only water. Then land. Then grass. Plants. Trees. Microbes. Ants. Rats. Apes... And then understand that all these exist in consciousness only. Any form has as its foundation, this sacred, magical and powerful Formless, in which it always exists.

How to get *it* out

The situation is that many people want to teach others, coach others, help others, advise others, and be consultants, trainers, facilitators or therapists. I prefer you to be a lover. A drunkard. At least become a musician or a poet. The world is in much greater need of these.

Soon, half the population will work and the other half will take care of them by offering training, massage, consultations, advice and many other things. Some trainers develop a weeklong program in which you can learn to jump over your own shadow.

That is great. When we help others, we help ourselves so it always works in all directions. However, always gauge your attitude.

It is interesting to teach, but are you also open to learn? When you give, do you also accept the gift?

There is no end to it: The more I give, the more I notice that there is to give.

Please do not think that you are finished in this school of life and mysticism. Always remain curious. There is always one step beyond! Have you pierced the mystery of time? Is your body totally stress-free? Where are you when the body sleeps? Are there no more 'uncooked seeds'? Is the mind totally settled? There are many phases of enlightenment, and most people haven't even glimpsed the first one yet. There are loading programs, upgrades, and siddhis. Don't be satisfied too quickly. Do you understand the mystery of the universe? Of sound? Have you pierced all the secrets of the body? Do you know how an angel, a deity, God and the Almighty are related? Are you aware of other life forms in the universe? Can you tap into the hidden knowledge? And certainly you don't have to. It is more than enough to lead a simple life. I just want to tell you that there are many layers of mysteries. It is almost unending.

So who is a 'sadhak'? A guru? A master? A tantrik? A yogi? A rishi? A Sage? The Perfect One?

It is true that we are all masters in a sense. Many people that I know have the potential to be a sage. But in order to be a guru, one needs to understand very well the difference between the real world and the unreal. A guru needs to speak from experience and not with, from or through book knowledge. One needs to understand precisely the effect of words and language and know their non-dual nature. One needs to have profound understanding of the veils including the veil of ignorance. A master is a true master. There are heavy qualifications for a sadhak and most readers are not meeting them (yet).

This whole game of spirituality is complicated in a sense because the master sees you firstly as a master. An equal. You are free. The only pity is that 'you' don't recognize this. You persistently operate behind the veils of ignorance, which aren't even real. You hold on to your false identity. You basically suffer from amnesia. You have forgotten your true nature and are now locked up in duality, identifying with a body. You are so proud of your personality and of the knowledge that your mind gathered over the years, chased by a relentless ego. The master basically says: "Step out of it!" and if you really did it and totally trusted him, it would be enough. But most doubters first need some proof and evidence.

It is very simple and yet also very understandable that this drives you nuts. It is also true that you need to learn to settle the mind. There are meditation techniques and mantras for that. But you should know what you are doing while meditating. You should know who is meditating and for what reason. Many people practise meditation to relax or to improve their health. That is insane. Of course it is not bad. Any reason that motivates people to meditate is fine, but it would be wiser to investigate our motivations. What are we hoping to get out of it? Who wants to get something out of it? I am trying to get *you* out of it, you see, and that is quite a different ball game!

But many people are not alert. Their mind is very drowsy. They need to wake up a bit more to the reality of life and therefore we shock and confront them. They feel very happy and proud but are in a hopeless situation really. Still hoping to get something. As if they are lacking something...

A Train of Thoughts

Krishnamurti was the rightful successor and was thus put in charge of the large and international organization that goes by the name of the Theosophical Society. Krishnamurti dismantled the entire organization as true spirituality does not need an *organization,* and of course he is totally right!

Sacrifice is to give up faith! That is the same as giving away the company of which you are the owner, and which was started by your great-grandfather and successively handed over to each next generation. Not an easy decision but for someone who is awake, VERY EASY. In Sufism, there are 'Rinds' and they abide by the law. Then, there are the wild ones like Hafiz. They break with the tradition and follow their own heart. These people cannot be imprisoned in an organization with lots of rules, politics, jealousy and stuff.

Understanding is the basis for wisdom while 'knowledge' only perpetuates ignorance. For all our knowledge to become fruitful, we need to know the Self. As a spiritual aspirant you need to be a bit naughty though. If everybody becomes very serious, the whole thing gets rather boring. You have to be serious in your practice however. I remember that when I studied at the university, I practised meditation every day for approximately three hours. I was also the president of the student society and drank three bottles of wine at a good party. And I was kicked out of school the most!

If spirituality becomes very serious, you know for sure that something is wrong. No person who is awake should take himself or herself too seriously. All these and more reasons make it challenging to have a 'spiritual' organization. It is almost a contradiction in terms.

That is why we have to be very aware. JC was a great man, but the church became a disaster. Even amidst a beautiful philosophy like Sufism – which is basically the same as the Path of Yoga, Beauty & Delight – these kinds of unfortunate things happen. But Tantra adapts to the changing times. Tantra is a mystery and you never know where the Shakti-energy is flowing. One needs to be keenly aware. Not get locked up with our gross senses in outer appearances. One can only trust the Heart and follow the Energy.

And you might be surprised to know that Anthroposophy derived from the Theosophical Society. Rudolf Steiner was the first of them. And the Theosophical Society is entirely based on the Tantra philosophy. You'd be very surprised by how the esoteric knowledge has been passed down in different ways throughout the ages.

We have desires and that is divine. If the Divine didn't have *desires* we would not be here. Some explain that we should suppress all our desires. Is that spirituality? NO. Tantra is to fulfil our desires until we find that chasing all these desires for ourselves is meaningless. And then we desire to serve other people and God, and become an instrument. A musical instrument.

At the last Olympics, again some records were broken and that is very exciting. But all records have been broken before and it always has been exciting. I know something that we can break which will be much more exciting still!

Have I explained to you there are three kinds of people around an ashram? Well, the truth is that there are many more, like parasites, but mainly we have ashramites, fans and visitors. Ashramites are the people who live there. Fans are people who wholly and holy support the place and come as often as possible, considering the obligations and responsibilities of work and family. Visitors are people who stay for one period because they want to learn how to play an instrument, have a burn-out, want to attend a program, need to recuperate, want to heal, learn something, or give birth to a child.

But what is the purpose of an ashram? They say it is a laundrette. It washes people extra quickly so to speak. All the impurities need to leave for you to have strong and clear recognition (pratyabhijna). The purpose is not to do rituals, but these rituals in the tantric tradition serve the purpose of love, peace, healing and wisdom. In the old days they would have been performed in a specific sacred place e.g. in the forest, but even that is difficult these days with the law. That is why I explained that the tree became a building and a book is the smoke coming from the fire. Where there is smoke, there is fire. Fire and heat cannot be separated. It is the nature of fire to give light.

We cannot say where the arm stops and where the hand starts. Where does the flame end and the smoke start? When did I start with this text?

- When I typed the first letter?
- When I selected 'new mail' on my menu?
- When I thought about it during running?
- When I opened my computer this morning?
- When I started the Tantra Mysticism e-group?
- When I was initiated?
- When I learned to meditate when I was 9?
- When I was born / conceived?
- When I first stumbled upon Kashmir Saivism several lifetimes ago?
- When I started to walk up straight a long time ago?
- When I became an animal?
- When I was infused with life for the first time?
- During the Big Bang?
- Or even before the previous cosmic dissolution?

So how long have we been related? When did the thought of separation occur for the first time?

- At your birth?
- When they told you about evil and sins?
- When you lost someone dear to you for the first time?
- When you became engrossed in a mind for the first time?

Were we ever not-related?

And when would this be?

Was there always a thread running through all the events in our life?

Where do we start when we trace this line back?

And go beyond even that?

Non-dualism is important. Tantra embraces duality and non-duality. Awareness transforms into consciousness. Consciousness transforms into the witness. The witness becomes the ego. The ego catches thoughts. A bundle of thoughts becomes a mind. The mind becomes entangled in the world-process. Kashmir Saivism explains this in much more detail and you can check it out for yourself.

Hardly anyone describes how this transformation takes place. And of course it is a mystery. Only the mind wants to know. Really you can just accept. This page has a back and a front. Can you see the back? Where is the back? What would you see if you look through the pages into the world of bits and bites? Einstein explained that energy is transformed into matter and that matter transforms into energy. We know from science that the building block of matter – an atom – consists of particles that are at the same time a wave. Sometimes the wave becomes a particle and vice versa. It even flickers in and out of existence. It disappears here and appears 'there'. It is as if on the edge of a black hole these tiny particles and waves go in and come out. The whole universe is on the verge of existence and non-existence. Can you balance your act on that edge?

The tantric liberation is just one of awareness and it is also the razor's edge. Complete awareness of Totality in the now. Many people wonder what the 'Here' and the 'Now' exactly are. It sounds spiritually cool but what is it exactly and why is it so difficult to be *there* (= Here!)? Here is no-place and Now is no-time. It is not easy to reside in no-time and no-place because you'll have to transcend everything and that requires very deep understanding. No mind can imagine how that is....

Only a no-mind truly experiences this without any imaginations. We imagine in our dreams. In dreams it is easy to imagine everything. The reality of ordinary waking state is hard to accept. We have many unfulfilled ambitions and desires that we act out during our dreams. In our dreams we can have a huge ashram. We can have nine wives and lots of money. This gives us a clue. The dream state is trying to prepare us for something. If it suddenly came into the waking state, it would be too shocking. The nervous system would not be able to handle it and cope with it.

The baby becomes a toddler. The toddler becomes a youth. The youth becomes a grown-up etc. The grown-up eventually becomes old and dies. All that he has gained, he cannot take with him. He only takes his unfulfilled desires and 'takes another incarnation'. That is why it is better to fulfil and work through all our desires. To realize the futility of all of them. To finally shake them all off and shake even our good friend 'death' off. Even he cannot 'catch' you anymore and you are welcomed by the Divine Mother.

Just as we cannot pinpoint when this writing exactly started and where the arm stops and the hand starts, we can also not say when the youth died and became a grown-up although it happened for sure as none of us are babies anymore. Or are we still? I guess so. I wish we all had the curiosity of a child. The same way consciousness becomes the witness or Iccha becomes Jnana. It does not, you see. Only a mind makes these kinds of assumptions. In Reality, it happens. It happens in a different way than we would describe with our mind. Oh yes, you can experience. And it is better that you experience for yourself. There is, unfortunately, nothing that guarantees that experience for you, but I would say that living in uncertainty is a very good bet. People who only have a couple of euros generally feel very much alive while those who are very wealthy tend to be rather dead!

One of the best *things* that can happen to you is when you lose your faith!

Why do you still carry that load? Is it so hard to become an explorer? Don't even have the ambition to become a master or a teacher. Let life happen. Just watch it going by and ENJOY!

What does this Path of Yoga, Beauty & Delight entail?

You'll have to be willing to step into the unknown. HOW TO DO THAT? You cannot simply 'step' into the unknown. Don't rely so much on the known however. Be willing to let go. Let things dissolve. Relinquish some of your attachments. Try to see things with a different eye. See things anew. You have to become worthy of the unknown. This mystery is only revealed to people who start to rely less on the senses and outer appearances. Try to see the hidden reality; the mystic and mythical domain. Disregard structure.

Let's not rely on book knowledge but let's see for ourselves. Most people on the spiritual path read too much. Whatever you want to get, cannot be got from reading books. It takes a mystic initiation. Drop the need to rely on books. Knowledge from the book stays in the book. Delve into the mysteries in the unconscious mind. They hold the secret passages.

It is about talking less and asking better questions. Silence is the key. Words are very misleading. Words will make circles in your mind. Excellent questions will bring you deeper within and strengthen the self-inquiry. What happens under the tree is determined by the quality of the questions that are asked.

An inquiry into the real nature of things and ourselves. In the spiritual inquiry it is very important to ascertain what the 'world' is made up of. What is the purpose of the existence on earth? What is my role in the larger picture? Who am I? What am I here for? What is 'my relationship' to the Divine?

A modern and un-dogmatic approach. This Yoga, Beauty & Delight is a very contemporary path. Left-handed Tantra uses 'the forbidden' par excellence. This however is under strict guidance of the guru. Yesterday I watched some MTV. The quality and creativity of some of these clips is quite impressive. A totally new form of art is arising, and it is these music clips. Some of the makers of these clips are obviously great artists. The use of colours and forms in some cases really 'pulls you in ... '. very lucid work!

Poetry over abstract and dry philosophy. Silence is the best. The real communion is in silence. Music is also a beautiful expression of Yoga, Beauty & Delight. Some poets are true artists in expressing the Inexpressible. The wisdom and the Shakti sometimes ooze off these pages. Yes, that is the deeper way to read. You read and drink the Shakti that is contained in these pages. Anyone can offer dry and intellectual philosophy. When our life is in danger, however, or we are confronted with huge problems in our life, we don't need 'philosophy' but we are in need of a helping hand or a comforting arm. That is the heart that can write poetry. Those are the gypsies and the courtesans on the Path of Yoga, Beauty & Delight. Always looking for hearts.

It is a radical approach. The matrix is a weird place. It is very seductive. It sucks you in. It holds you prisoner. A prisoner of your mind! You keep on runnin' around and around looking for something that cannot be found there. Why not? Because it is HERE! It is on the other side and the most important thing you can do is to find a boatman who is willing to take you across. You can accomplish all kinds of things in the matrix but it is just like building a sandcastle. One day, a wave will come and this wave will take the entire sandcastle back to the sea. It is nice to build sandcastles – don't get me wrong. But I am here to stimulate you to open your eyes to a much deeper reality of life. BUT....

It is for those who are thirsty and hungry.... You need to be very thirsty. Curiosity is a good trait when it is combined with thirst! The thirst comes when you find out that what you are looking for cannot be found in the matrix. This is the state that Neo was in. He started to question and to doubt the 'reality' he was living in. He knew there was something more to life. You have to set out for the Truth!

Alchemy. Yes... Tantra and this School of Yoga, Beauty & Delight are **alchemy** indeed. Of course, nobody can sanely explain to you what 'alchemy' is. It is a secret and hidden science. You might come to know a bit more over time. Many alchemists never had an official training. It just came to them. And not 'just' of course! I have also warned you many times that this path is difficult and not without danger, and this is not just written as a joke. A wrong mixture and there is a slight explosion in the lab...

A complete human being. Not that we are not complete, although we are in a way. Some things need to be processed. Some seeds need to sprout or to cook. Unresolved things need to be resolved. Purusha and Prakriti need to be blended. It is still a great mystery what this 'purusha' and 'prakriti' is. We will get to it. Osho talked about Zorba the Buddha. The yogin and the bhogin combined in one person. The man who could be totally still and detached, totally immersed in Essence and the man who could dance and enjoy. But he danced in multi-dimensional consciousness! Similar concept to the Shiva Nataraj. The great and charming Cosmic Dancer who crushes the dwarf of ignorance under his feet while performing his magnificent dance.

Delving into the mysteries of the unconscious mind. I am not only talking about therapy. It is also a matter of self-inquiry. It is mainly an exploration. An exploration in consciousness. It is not a rational thing that I am going to accomplish in a three-year training period. Maybe there will be no end to it. This world is not a Newtonian model. It only looks as if some things are predictable. Come to accept life as a mystery. But only when you have drowned.

Piercing the metaphysics. One of the last stages is the metaphysics. There are so many secrets... It is interesting to develop our full capabilities. Why are there so few Michelangelos these days? Everybody is specialized in this or that. Yet my friend Paul du Marchie, whom I have spent some time with every year for 25 years now, masters many forms of art and science. He built his own house in Switzerland. It is built in a medieval style. He made every door by himself, every lock. He lectures in astronomy. He is an expert on Nietzsche. Repairs clocks and watches. Speaks seven languages. Paul spent many years in monasteries like Mt. Athos. He is an expert in Egyptian art and lived for five years in Egypt. He led caravans through the desert and lived with the Touaregs. Paul and his wife built a crypt underneath their house with the same smell, temperature and humidity as the King's chamber in the pyramid of Cheops. He built one of the largest church organs in Europe in the part of his house in the mountain (only 1/3 of the house is visible from the outside). He has also mastered most of the ancient arts like blowing glass, making stained glass, medieval writing, working with gold, making Russian icons etc. He also fought in Afghanistan decades ago. What a human being can do is amazing. Unfortunately most people squander their lives aimlessly in the matrix....

Strongly embracing all sorts of Arts. Many people are engrossed in business and they have hardly developed an eye for the arts. Or an ear to hear 3-D. Why? What is so interesting to attain through business? You wanna get wealthy? Provide yourself with security? What kind of 'security'? Don't you know what the current state of affairs is? The whole economy is a balloon. The whole world is like Enron. I hear many spiritual people say that they want to make a lot of money and then later give it away for spiritual purposes. But I can tell you that if you don't develop the habit of giving away now, it'll only get worse later on. You'll become very attached. Your business side will corrupt you.

Enjoy dance. Not looking at it, but **dancing and moving your hips**. Free the energy that is stored there. Many spiritual approaches work from the fourth chakra and up. For me it is imperative that you work the whole body. Many people have strong issues with sexuality. They have to be worked through and that is why we have floors number 1, 2 and 3. You cannot develop the nobility that is necessary by suppressing your sexuality. It is a mighty strong force. And this society is not really doing us any 'good' with all sorts of crazy and unnatural ideas that are forced upon us. We need to free whatever is locked up in our hips. That is where the Kundalini Shakti is stored. She is asleep and you ought to to become an excellent belly dancer. You need to be able to rotate your hips AND enjoy it. There is enough room in your life later on to sit silently.

It is really **an exploration into the Unknown.** That is what this path is and you are the explorer. We can help/inspire each other but it is an individual journey. There are risks in any undertaking and you need to travel well prepared. At one point, I can guarantee you that you will find somebody who is waiting for you and has been waiting for you a long time.

It is not only reading these chapters with your mind but also trying to tune in and feel the energy. Tantra is mostly about energy. Sending and receiving energy. Understanding how energy transforms, transmutes, transmits and trance-mutates. Can you make contact in the astral realm? For this you'll have to develop a very strong steadiness and you need to develop your antennae. The conditions are very favourable, but you are the one who has to do it (or not do it).

It is about tuning in, taking silence, being in nature, meditating, dancing, singing and celebrating. The task at hand is enormous, as I described. We are setting out on a great journey. It might take many years, decades or lifetimes. The journey is not a cerebral one. It is your head (ego) that you need to offer. Contemplate this well. You can only move forward when you are ready and some people are linked to each other in destiny. It is a Magic Carpet of love that we are weaving. Enlightenment is not an individual effort.

It is about wildness and ecstasy. Even though this ship is the Ishvara-ship and we have set out on a spiritual quest, I insist that we don't become too serious. In fact it is not 'even though' but it is BECAUSE! Because this ship is the Ishvara ship and because of the enchantment of the Lila of the great Lord, we should dare to be wild and roam around in ecstasy. Some of you can surely improve on this one. Make sure you have a zest for life. Immerse yourself in it as well! But try/work to remain aware. Trance dancing is very useful!

It is also about stillness, quietness and silence. Mostly, it is about this. But when the mind is restless – as is the case with most people – it is also good to move and to exhaust yourself. Don't be afraid of the extremes. It is often the case that because we were willing to sail the extremes, we find the balance in the middle. And even though we were there before, this balance is now much more meaningful and rich.

It is embracing the paradox. The divine mystery of life. Keen readers have discovered that I write paradoxes almost all the time. Paradoxes – like koans – are hard for the mind. That is the exact reason that I offer them to you. Figure it all out.

Don't try to understand it all but accept that life is a mystery. That means that you have to squeeze out the essence. You start with the 'in-essence'. It is difficult to understand all of the 'in-essence' but you can try and make a start. The Essence is very easy to process. Very natural.

Not to suppress and not to indulge. If you have to choose one of these two, I would rather that you go too much with indulgence. Experiencing it all will help you to become more detached later on. At the end of his life they asked Mulla Nasrudin whether he would commit all his sins and mistakes again, were he to live his life all over. Nasrudin answered that he would surely commit all of them and many more, and that he would start with it much earlier in life!

There is no 'success' to be gained but wisdom to be given. I am still afraid that some people, if they were offered a boon and they could choose between wealth or wisdom, would make the wrong choice... But then fortunately there is no 'wrong' choice and we can also use some wealth in this School of Yoga, Beauty & Delight, as we want to set up a beautiful and large ashram where many of you can live, work and play. An ashram where families and children are also welcome. A place to heal, rejuvenate, do inquiry and where a lot of wine is poured to all thirsty travellers.

I really have all my hopes on the young people. These children are so beautiful, so wise. I really pray that we as adults don't screw up their lives. That is the reason why you must do all you can to develop ourselves. If you have many 'defects' you'll pass them on to your children. Personal development will heal you and help you to become more whole. Not that you are not whole, but we suffer from amnesia and have forgotten our divine nature. That is why human beings engage in nasty things.

I would not even want to have children (personally) until I know of an excellent school where I can send them. So we need to start this ashram and then expand with a school in Yoga, Beauty & Delight. It can really not be done any other way. All of you who have children notice how difficult the situation is. We do not only need the building (and the permits) but we need teachers. Capital and excellent teachers. Some of you, I guess. These are among the reasons that I insist that you take things that I write seriously and make a superhuman effort to understand these messages in all their depth.

Some people shop around a lot and everybody is free to do whatever they want, but in the traditions from the East it really doesn't work that way. That is just a part of the Western schizophrenia; the fear of missing out and the fear of being hurt. It is a sign of immaturity. You can study with whomever you want. There are beautiful teachers out there. Even though some teach things like you can manifest whatever you intend or desire, and even though anyone with a sane mind can conclude that that is utter non-sense, I am OK with your studying and taking on more and becoming more and more confused. I also was once confused. I also studied many, many things. I was involved with many schools and teachings. My thirst was almost unquenchable. I followed a thread however! And I can tell you that this Tantra philosophy and this School of Yoga, Beauty & Delight will give you all that you want, dream and hope for. But don't believe me. You need to find out for yourself. And if you first want to roam around that is fine with me.

My writings are very clear. It is clear with whom I can continue and with whom not. They will experience a different trip although we appear to be on the same boat.

Most of the world religions are based on the dichotomy of the mind. Most people will cling to dualism, as this is the philosophy of the mind. The mind experiences everything as dual. The mind identifies. It identifies with the body and with a false concept of who we are. It lives in a world of appearances. The mind thinks itself to be very clever and the mind is even proud of itself that it engages in 'spiritual growth'. There is however no thorough awakening using the mind as the unseen core to which we attach our spiritual growth.

The mind is heavily conditioned. The mind stores memories and pain. It tries to protect. The mind is a very finite and limited instrument.

Yesterday, I saw a movie about a professor who won the Nobel Prize at a late age for a breakthrough. In his younger days he was a pioneer in mathematics. He was schizophrenic all of his life. In his speech he said that he travelled through all these domains including the metaphysics and came back again. But then you don't come back the same. It is like you travelled with the Lords of the Rings. You've met Ellie in the Vanilla Sky. You know about Zu. You understand the Matrix. You know where platform 9 3/4 is.

Mirdad didn't speak for seven years while he was already a great master. In Kali Yuga, the deaf will lead the blind. Alchemy is not an easy subject. In the mystic realm the laws are rather different than in the matrix and most human beings are fairly impatient.

Mind-mastery implies that we learn to settle down the mind. It takes many years of practice. Diligence. Patience. Surely, we can all help each other and ourselves. Be open. Never lose your curiosity. Please always remember what I have said so many times: The more I experience, the more I experience there is to experience!

No philosophy out of a book will bring you there. You need to be contacted by a boatman in the inner realm. The answers will come.

Relating, Relationships and the Sins committed

We are all related and in the physical realm we relate to many people. There seems to be such turmoil. Communication requires the mind, and that un-purified mind causes some trouble. It is not objective. It projects. It has fears and desires. There are games, blame and power struggles. There is no full responsibility. It is a situation of weakness.

Most people are concerned about their love relationships. There is a deep longing for our soul-mate. We long to re-unite and look for a solution in form. That is fine. There is no problem with that. I am certainly not suggesting that we are going to live by ourselves under a separate tree with no interaction! In the Path of Yoga, Beauty & Delight this interaction is very important. It challenges us to see and to recognize the Divine in everything and everyone, everywhere and at all times.

Now...this is easier said than done. Yoga is a path, as in a practice, and it is also the goal, as in 'unity'. As 'a practice' we make effort to see the Divine in everyone. That is why we bow with respect to another person and say 'Namaste'; I greet the Divinity in you! Also we take on other practices by which we purify the mind. The more purified, the more we can see (the more I can see, the more I see there is to see!). The better we hear. Our senses become much wider, more open and receptive. Also our touch becomes subtler.

Sincere practice has to be done under guidance. If you really want to make progress in the spiritual realm, the best you can do is to find a guide, a preceptor. There is only so much you can do by yourself to purify. The ultimate purification comes by Divine Grace. When Divine Grace showers upon you at last, all the knots are untied. At that point it is effortless. It is the Reality.

Even a master who lives in total and non-dual awareness may interact with people and engage in communication. This master will foremost see the divine flame in other people. His/her heart overflows with love. Depending on his 'task' and 'training' (dharma), he may work with people on their personality in an outer form or not. 'Outer form' here, means through verbalisation etc. There are other ways!

But back to us, living in the earthly realm. We who long to re-unite with our soul mate and screw up our relationships. What to do? We need to practise detached involvement. You are involved. That, you already are. Now, you stay involved but add some more wisdom. Infuse your relationships with awareness. It has never been said that it would be easy. Practise a bit more detachment. Let go of your needs. You need this and that. Inquire into them and come to more acceptance. You are not placed on this planet to change everybody and to mould him or her into your ideas of right and wrong. Make yourself less important.

Let things happen as they happen. What is your 'problem'? Your problem is (in) your mind. There is no sane, healthy or loving relationship possible as long as you rely on your mind. The mind is the projector of duality. Duality equals ignorance, conflict and war. You have all sorts of models in your head. You have rules and expect people to behave like this or that and they don't. So where is the pain and the suffering? Can you point your finger to it? I am sure you can!

You are a conditioned automaton with crazy ideas of how the world is supposed to be. Who invented 'marriage'? Marriage is a curse and a blessing at the same time. There is nothing wrong with marriage. Marriage is a wonderful thing. The problem is the rules and expectations that your mind imposes on it. Now you feel that you 'own' this person and that he or she owes you something or vice versa. This false feeling of ownership is the problem. That is why – in this sadhana – you have to let go of all ideas of ownership.

Most people don't own the most important thing they possess. In fact they are not even aware of their infinite treasure. And they want to own things that are non-essential. They long to own the false. They have very strong attachment to illusion. They are very proud of their matrix-toys. Not willing to let go of the fantastic possessions that the ego won during difficult battles on planet earth, in which they had to cheat others and lie to themselves. Which corrupted them as human beings into worshipping the golden calf.

And now we complain how hard it is to relate to people. I wonder why...?
This is what happened to the heroism of mankind. We're running around after our own pleasures, defending what is ours. Not willing to let go, or even to share. Turning it all into a great show of power. The most powerful and 'influential' figures are portrayed in the media as the successful ones. They have become the new heroes. The most ignorant ones, devoid of wisdom. They haven't even figured out yet that we do not really own anything and that we are here together on the planet to share!

Can you see those tendencies in yourself? Who are you corrupting with your ideas and lies? Is it so hard to see the unity in diversity? The diversity is beautiful! The world is beautiful. When we come to acceptance and to loving each other. When we want to share what we've got. Especially when we focus on giving. The real heroes are ready to give away even their clothes, our final 'possession', and to stand naked. They are the people we admire. We celebrate their birthday or death. But we forget all about the deeper meaning and now eat dead turkey on those holy days!

I am all in favour of restoring nobleness. Holidays were meant to be holy days I guess, but we spend them on Tenerife. We all desire to be liberated. We want to be free. Some people sense that maybe through this involvement with Ralph, some day they will get to partake in a tantric ritual with many people. But my dear friends what are you willing to sacrifice? What are you willing to offer? And I am not talking about goats! I want to see your blood dripping because of a personal wound. A willingness to suffer. Letting go is not letting go of the superfluous. Everything that is false is superfluous.

So you ask me whether it is any wonder that so many people have relationship challenges? You want to grow spiritually but have not figured out yet that there is nothing to gain. It is not at all about reading nice books or going to lectures of some charismatic lunatic who also has read many books. From such a person you will indeed gain a lot. But do you want that? That is why I say so many times that you have to be very aware of what it is that you want! Most of you want something. You desire a gain while I say that there is no-thing to gain. You will be better off when you lose. But you are afraid to lose because you are conditioned into how wonderful it is to be successful.

Is it so wonderful? You know what is really full of wonder? Your nakedness. When you are naked you are wonderful. But you prefer to dress yourself with the latest fashions and expensive jewellery. There is nothing wrong with that except when you try to cover your nakedness. I love beauty and you need to accept yourself as beauty-full. You are beauty and you are full of beauty; how else can we say that the world is beautiful? Can you undress yourself and strip yourself naked, looking at yourself in the mirror and smiling all the way? Without any pretence?

Because then, the clothes will look much more beautiful on you. You are a daughter or a son of the Divine Mother.

Masks are beautiful. But not when you are totally identified with them. You are the Mother Kali (as a woman). You are the Shiva (as a man). You are not even only a man or a woman. You are both and even more than that. It is fine to walk around in this body but you are not it. You are a divine pulsation. But it is useless to say these things when people are shrouded in

ignorance. It is this ignorance that I choose to start with. My focus as Ralph is not on telling you about the Divinity but to help you to pierce the ignorance. I am ready to travel with you through the underworld. On the back of the devil if necessary. Let's shake this 'thing' off. I desire to dance with you and crush the ignorance.
Go wild and laugh in ecstasy. To make love and shake the duality. To shake and to let go. Shake and let go. But never forget that the way to drive away the darkness is to introduce light.

There are many issues stored in the body and it is important to work through the body. Get some firm and good bodywork. Twice per week if you can. Abhinavagupta – the towering giant in non-dualistic Kashmir Saivism – said that when you have pierced all the secrets in and of the body, you have pierced all the secrets in the entire Universe, as they are not separated from each other.
So we can start far away or really close by and I suggest the last. You don't even have to move your arm. You don't even have to wink to discover the true abode. The Wisdom Goddess. JC: 'The Kingdom of Heaven is within'. These words were spoken by a man who did not want an organisation and surely not a church. You see the rape is all around us. See the world religions for what they are doing. Are they suppressing people or liberating them? So where is the anti-Christ?

Look at all these churches and mosques.... They are beautiful buildings but nothing particularly divine is happening there. You and your body are divine. And for that reason wherever they are is a divine place.

Media, Power and the Goddess

The media train us well. On TV, in newspapers and magazines we see and read about our modern day heroes. These heroes are not much like Perseus and Odysseus. The heroes of today are moneymakers. Famous singers, dancers, actors and wealthy businessmen. I often wonder why we are so amused by these wealthy people and even want to be like them. What is it in the glamour and glitter that attracts us?

Maybe it is the light....

And we want very much to be like them. We strive to be successful. We are willing to corrupt and to manipulate in order to make a move upward. We negotiate and make concessions. We join the game of politics. We fight to defend our position and what we consider to be ours. We sacrificed a lot to attain it. We sacrificed our lives and became machines. A machine programmed for 'success'. We want more and refuse less. The only way is up! We strive to enlarge our 'kingdom'. We increase taxes. The more successful we become, the more we lose our bonds with our past friends. Poverty attracts us no more.

We associate with our newly found friends. Especially, we welcome 'hypocrisy' although we do not immediately recognize him at every party...

In Tantra philosophy, we worship the Goddess. The wisdom-Goddess. Our hero is not the successful one. That fruit carries too heavy a price. The boon of the Goddess is wisdom. Wisdom is priceless. It cannot be bought. No book can bestow it upon you. It is not contained in education. It cannot be gained by study. Study is in the realm of the mind. One who approaches Tantra with his mind, may certainly become a good student and even write books about Tantra like so many have done, but he or she will not understand what it is to be a devotee. Only a master holds the keys that are necessary to go deeper within.

A disciple sets out to enter a relationship in the heart. She is willing to surrender. To bear loss. A disciple is willing to sacrifice her life. She welcomes the mystery and is not looking to affirm the known. Sometimes the gain comes with the loss. A disciple understands the principle of letting go. A disciple is willing to go with the flow. To surrender to the Almighty. Let Thy Will Be Done! That is a beautiful mantra. A disciple is ready to sacrifice her own desires and attachments to the fire. The fire that eats and devours everything that is offered into it. The fire of consciousness. The disciple longs to ignite that fire in her heart.

Feeling the burning sensation of separation from the Beloved. That gives rise to the longing. The yearning. She drags herself to the Divine Tavern where the innkeeper might pour her a drink. A drink of illumination. This is the light that the disciple prefers over the fake light of glamour and glitter. This disciple is unwavering. She has discovered the perfect relationship. A relationship of unbounded joy and ecstasy. I can no longer hide from the Beloved. No matter what mask I wear. She always recognizes me. So I choose to dress up and prepare myself.

It is better to abstain from the opium of the news and the church, my friends. Your stomach is too full and makes you lazy. You cannot even think clearly anymore. The opium that the church of the poisoned mind gives away is not for free. It comes at a heavy price, which is imprisonment. A prison of duality; caught amidst 'good' and 'evil'. Be careful of what it is that you want. Whatever you desire is the God(dess) that you worship. When you desire wealth, you worship the Goddess of wealth. In the same way you can worship the Goddess of beauty.

And what are your offerings? What are you willing to sacrifice? What is the price you have paid and are willing to pay?

At some point in time, man seized the power and forgot how to worship the Goddess and women in the proper way. All religions turned masculine. The male dominion ruled the world. And look outside (and inside!). We see war, separation, struggle, and conflict. This was not the case when the feminine spirit 'ruled' with love, peace, harmony and understanding. The governments are male. The boards and directors are male. The Vatican is male. Maybe here and there, there are some women but mostly they have been corrupted and are more male than female.

Only Tantra has kept the secret alive. It kept the flame burning for many thousands of years. In the past, there were temple priestesses that taught men (about) love. JC worshipped all women. But of course the totally fundamentalist disciples were heavily discriminating against women. In those days, women were only good for making food and having children, and they should surely not be involved in religion, 'spirituality' or philosophy. Men may know about religion and philosophy but those are matters of the mind. They turned religion into a battlefield. Look at any war that is presently going on and you will find that they are all based on religious conflicts. Conflicts arising out of religious superiority.

Many, many countries have invaded India. The people allowed the enemy to enter and they hardly ever defended themselves properly. Many enemies came, 'conquered' and went. India was never expansionist. It never invaded other countries. Invasion and expansion are typical male traits. As are fundamentalism and evangelism. As are corruption and competition. Oppression and suppression. Every man comes out of a woman but he forgets to pay tribute to the Divine Mother, and now the world is bleeding and continues to bleed. The earth will restore itself, but what is to become of the human race?

When these are our heroes?

I invite you to contemplate which Goddess you worship and what your worship is.

In the old days, men protected their women. And look what happens when you protect or even worship the women in your life. The boon is that you will become a man. And the women have so much to give and to share. But they have been so busy protecting themselves against men. It is sometimes quite a struggle... The shadow has a devastating effect on both. But through self-inquiry and tantric sadhana the flame starts to burn brighter. The light of awareness reaches even the far away hidden corners of our subconscious mind.

And then we discover that there is so much love. Look at the many women on this ship. The ship almost sails effortlessly. It is under divine guidance. Tantra must be practised under divine guidance, as is the way in Sufism. We are dealing with mighty forces and our lives can be swept in any direction. It is because of the feminine spirit that the ship sails with so much love, compassion, tolerance, openness and peace. There is an inner attunement.

I sincerely thank my guru and the guiding light in my and our life for all the blessings and guidance. He who sacrifices his life – like Morpheus – to save ours. We, who do not even know that we need to be saved. We, who do not even realise how badly we need help. And he keeps on giving. Shining his light of protection. And even though our surrender is so weak... Even though we are so stubborn... Despite our pride... And our unsteadiness... Even though we are so shallow, he keeps on pouring the depths. This fountain is never-ending. Grace keeps on showering forth. Even though we do not show the proper gratitude. Even though we are ignorant of what is happening. Even though our sadhana is so weak.

We are all eternally indebted and we will only realize this when it is too late. Not too late for us, because it will never be too late for us. I guess this is how it goes, but surely hope that wisdom will rise sooner rather than later for us. Mankind is engrossed in ignorance and it is hard to recognize a helping hand. A sword carried by a hand that knows how to cut, but not how to reflect the light of the sun on its blade, will even cut off the hand of the son of the sun. May the Lord guide us!

Adversaries

Some people tend to think that the more they progress on the spiritual path (if such a thing were possible), the better their life will become. Meaning that there will be more bliss, things will get better, they will be more able to create the life they want, they will prosper more and be happier in their relationships.

Is the reverse also true? What does it mean when things are not going as we intended? Why do so many people have serious challenges in their relationships? How come some very spiritual people have already been yearning to find their soul mate for many years?

What does this have to do with the fact that many people have a hang-up about 'the guru'? A hang-up in the sense that they resist the idea of a guru and don't want anything to do with it OR they are totally in an unhealthy adoration state about 'the guru' in form.

Yet, we also know that in order to make progress in any field, we need a guide or a teacher. In order to learn how to play the violin, we need a teacher. It would be hard to learn it via a CD-ROM. In order to become a good carpenter, we need to work together with a master in carpentry for some years. To become a good coach, we need to spend many months with a wizard in coaching. When we spend time with a great and wise captain, we will learn not only how to steer a ship but also about handling other affairs.

So what is the resistance against a spiritual teacher when someone is very thirsty to make progress in the spiritual arena? How come it is so hard to establish who is a valid teacher in spirituality? Why is a relationship with a master in spirituality so 'difficult'? And why is it so that once people enter into a relationship with a (spiritual) master, they often lose their common sense and go into oblivion? What is real and healthy devotion?

The job of the real master is not to impart spiritual knowledge. The master will simply shake you. That is what he or she does and will do. But in order to really shake you, there must be a very strong bond. In the process of shaking, resistance, confrontation, anger, jealousy, confusion and shame will arise and much more. They have to be processed and investigated. The disciple needs to already have some maturity. The disciple must know how to be silent. Not to talk too much and not to lose him- or herself in a myriad of projections. To enter into a relationship with a tantric master is not without 'risk'.

Now, to come back to the first question that I raised. Is it the case that progress in the spiritual arena goes together with a more harmonious life? I have just explained how that is not necessarily the case. The life of JC was not easy in the beginning, not in the middle and not at the end, although we do not really know how the end was. Supposedly Jesus died and was buried in Kashmir at a late age (in his seventies/eighties).

We need to investigate all of our beliefs and thought concepts. The most interesting are our ideas on 'spirituality'. There we very often find the biggest mess. An even bigger mess than our ideas about our relationships, although we do a good job over there too.

Spirituality has a lot to do with acceptance. Acceptance is a whole different ball game from the new age idea of creating the reality that we want. That is nice for kindergarten. But we have to mature. Maturing is not very easy for a child who was comforted at the breast every time he or she cried. This stimulus-response created infantile grandiosity meaning we believe that we can suck a breast every time we play a trick.

Infantile grandiosity is a disease many people of the Western population suffer from. It has already created a huge and very bad virus on the planet. It is the typical matrix idea that we can change the matrix. But it is still not clear to us who created the matrix. That is a very difficult question in the movie The Matrix*. That is why we have to do very deep inquiry. What I present in this book is depth psychology and philosophy (no-mind philosophy also using Twilight Language). You are the one who has to do some very serious contemplation. You need to find the answers by yourself.

That is also what Morpheus told Neo: "Relax! The answers will slowly come by themselves". We can't have all the answers at once. The ultimate is so shocking that you need to be slowly – very slowly! – prepared. And he took Neo on quite a training program...

Neo was ready. Very ready! And he still had to throw up. He couldn't believe it when he 'started to see it'. Morpheus explained: "The mind has trouble letting go!" They carefully selected Neo especially. Morpheus had high expectations of him. Neo possessed a certain talent. A talent that he himself was as yet unaware of. A talent and a power to free the world. It is not clear from the movie whether Neo is the only person who has that talent. The movie makes us believe that that is the case. It all depends on who the One is. Neo is the One (NEO → ONE).

As you may remember from the movie, Neo couldn't sleep at night. When Trinity found him in the discotheque (in the matrix, meaning she had to go in), she told him that she knew him very well. That she knew why he couldn't sleep at night. Because he was looking for something. That something is the answer to the question. Do you my dear readers recall what that question is?

There are some movies that are interesting to study in depth. We all have a job. But the one thing that we do not all have, and that we do not share equally, is our thirst. And Neo had that incredible thirst and THAT is the reason why Morpheus could work very well with him. Neo could not even sleep at night; he was trying so hard to contemplate. He didn't go to parties to waste his time. He was doing some very serious sadhana. And anyone who does very serious sadhana will find a Morpheus.

The wife of Shiva (Shakti) was born anew as the daughter of the Himalayas. Her name was Himvati. Also known as Uma or Parvati. Through her entire youth, she only thought about

Shiva. Nothing else interested her. Even as a young girl she did very strong sadhana. She became an incredibly beautiful girl. Many people and Gods tried to tempt her, but her mind was firmly established on Shiva. Brahma had already predicted that she was to marry Shiva and that from their marriage a son would be born who would defeat the army of the demons (a similar task to Neo's). Uma was meditating for many years in the forest. She created such a strong field of energy that Shiva noticed it in his cave in the Himalayas. He could not ignore it or her any longer and he tested her. Very difficult tests. Virtually impossible to succeed, but she did and they finally married.

This means that Shiva (Grace) will come to anyone who practises strong sadhana and He will marry (merge or unite with) him or her. Shiva will not come to those who talk a lot. Not to the lazy ones. Not to those whose mind is very unsteady. Not to those who do not practise (awareness), although He might. In general this is the way: to practise strong sadhana and to build your field of energy. To kindle the inner flame and to allow a mighty fire to arise. It is the guru who ignites this flame in tantric sadhana. This Path of Yoga, Beauty & Delight is not the talking-school. I am not interested in semi-Tantra. Let the deaf lead the blind. Tantra is a very serious practice and you must be willing to do the homework. In the beginning the guru always gives some very small tasks and homework. Very easy to do for anyone. And then he checks how serious people are, and unfortunately it is usually the case that only very few people have some discipline.

For Tantra one needs good discipline. Tantra is for the vira. The serious practitioner. Tantra is a very noble way of life. It is not for those who are just after sheer pleasure. Tantra embraces pleasure all right. That is also very important to understand. Dance, music, lovemaking and ecstasy are very important ingredients on this Path of Yoga, Beauty & Delight. We are still at the beginning. The circumstances are not yet there to go any deeper in our experience of Tantra. Most people are still too engrossed in their lives, The matrix and their mind. There is a very low willingness to sacrifice and to let go, even among the sailors on our ship. Arrogance is bigger than the thirst.

If someone tells Paul du Marchie that, according to Feng Shui, he should place his bed to the North but certainly not to the West, Paul will surely place his bed to the West! The strongest force on this planet is gravity. It is people like Paul whose life is the story of someone who refuses to go with the gravity. We may have many adversaries in our life. Paul certainly had his share as you can read in his book.

It is not philosophy that will come to the aid of mankind but dance, music, ecstasy and Divine Madness. I invite the tantric energy to enter our heart and soul. Let it bewilder our minds and infuse our bodies. What most people consider to be sane is from my/our perspective totally insane. I long to be lost in rapture. Let the sword of Mercy hit hard on/in the neck of those who are ignorant. I am willing to sharpen the saw. This ship is not for lazy folk who are ignorant and peep at the wild women danc~~ing on~~ this ship, secretly masturbating. Everyone needs to become a dancer of life. It is the only way to step away from the gravity. Hear the divine melody. Feel the pulsation in your hips. Allow yourself to be taken. Dare to lose yourself in ecstasy. Drink from the wine that the capitane is pouring. Don't walk all your life behind a farting camel. Climb on the chariot and take the reigns. Steer your horses to drink from the well. Become saturated with Divine Madness.

* The Matrix part 1

The Doctrine of Acceptance

Why is this Acceptance so hard?

Do we imagine ourselves to be superior? If we were in charge would we do it better?

'Life is not fair and we need to change it.' We do not want to be a master of ourselves, but we want to become a master of life. Without fulfilling the needed requirements or 'paying the ticket'.

What and who really is a master of life?

What does that entail and imply?

Many masters have demonstrated what it is. In our Christian tradition there are so many beautiful examples.

Have you sometimes prayed to God begging to take over the suffering from/of someone else? I am sure most of you have. Then there is no complaining!

In that case, it is your obligation to accept things as they are. You must accept sickness, disease, misfortune and poverty.

So why would you set out to create the desired reality?

It might be more intelligent to investigate in whose *reality* you are living right now. Which part of it is the reality of your parents? Of advertisers? Do you prefer a slim woman to a 'fat' woman? Different cultures have different ideas about 'fat' and 'slim'. And your ideas about beauty are heavily influenced by advertising. How much do you live in the reality of the church with ideas of sin, heaven and hell? Before we set out to create something, it is much wiser to establish where you are. In order to travel to 'a desired reality' we need to know from where we are departing. If we really pierce our current reality and go to the bottom of it, it is likely that your present situation will become close to your desired reality.

Is it the case that if someone sets out to create the desired reality that he or she does not accept the present or current situation?

Part of the training in YB&D is to learn to be grateful for everything. Contemplate this well! Most people are grateful when something happens that they want. They want one thing and do not want another thing. Being grateful for everything that happens in your life is a great lesson and a tough task to master.

Does that mean we become passive? NO!

Being passive is not at all the outcome of this philosophy.

The Path of Yoga, Beauty & Delight – like non-dual Kashmir Saivism – is a path of the heart. It resides in an open heart. It blooms on compassion. It is fertilized with discipline. It brings forth sweet and strong fragrances by earnest and sincere work and sadhana (spiritual practice). Spiritual practice must always be based on acceptance.

What does that mean for our work? Work is very important. We strive to do our work as well as we can. We do not get involved in power games, nor do we engage in gossip. We are loyal towards the organization we work for and to our employer. But you do your work with awareness. This is VERY difficult. Much more difficult than most people can imagine. 'With awareness' means every gesture, every word. No distractions to the past or the future and no projections. That is worship. Then our life becomes very beautiful and joyful. The grass is only greener on the other side when viewed from the mind. Outside of the mind, our life is a meditation and every action is worship. Only in the mind is there duality. Duality is glued together with conflict, desires and un-fulfilment.

One of the sentences that I often use: In the ocean of desires there is no island called fulfilment.

Most people want fulfilment but they will even have to let go of wanting and seeking. That which we are seeking cannot be found because it is not outside of us. Around us is spun the matrix-world. We need to investigate it for what it is worth. You need to see that for yourself. I cannot explain it to you. You need to experience it. In order to experience it you need to investigate the glasses through which you are looking. As long as you wear coloured glasses, you cannot see the world objectively. This means that you will have to learn to see the world with closed eyes, as our eyes are the thieves. They are the deceivers. But what remains of the world when we withdraw our senses?

You'll have to come to the understanding that science is only worth so much. Philosophy is another thing and religion another again. The scientists, philosophers and the priests are all fairly convinced of themselves. Bush calls Iran demonic and for the people from Iran the US is satanic. The good is located within and the bad is usually located 'outside'. This is the attitude of a coward.

But before we judge the outside, we need to understand the process of perception very well. And even many people who explain how perception works, still have a gross and fragmented understanding. We need to understand how awareness transforms into consciousness. How the ego arises out of this and how thoughts are received. The functioning of the mind. We have to understand very precisely how we function in what is called the waking state. We need to understand the dream-state and why it is much easier to feel fulfilled in the dream-state. And then we need to understand the mystery of the sleeping state. Then we need to figure out how to awake from all of those and to become the watcher.

We can also take a detour into the wilderness of creating our desired destiny. But I suggest we go straight to the source. You will have to do some deep inquiry for that.

That is why this text was on **the Doctrine** of Acceptance!

It is only upon acceptance that we can LET GO!

Beyond the Witness

I have explained previously that Awareness transforms into Consciousness. Consciousness transforms into the Witness. Out of this the whole world arises with the ego. How do the rishis know all of this?

Because they followed the tattvas back, experiencing deeper and more profound levels of enlightenment and illumination. The same is possible for all of you readers when you stop reading and start to drink.

Tantra also means movement.

In the state of pure, undivided and unqualified awareness, which we call Shiva, there is a slight movement. A movement that is not a movement. We call this Spanda.

Many people understand Tantra to have something to do with freedom, beauty & delight. When I describe our school as The Path of Yoga, Beauty & Delight I write with capital letters. Why? Because we are talking about the most beautiful. The most delightful. What is the most liberating? Most liberating is pure knowledge. Tantriks worship the wisdom-Goddess. The ignorant strive after earthly success. To the wise that is pretty meaningless. Success is never lasting. 'Success' comes with a heavy price. History has proved that success goes up and down like the tides. People try to catch success, but the truth is that they are in the clutches of it.

I advised you to watch some particular movies to open yourself for the investigation into reality. The question keeping Neo awake at night was: "What is the matrix?" The matrix is maya. The matrix consists of opposites. Maya is duality: black & white, night & day, ebb & flow, profit & loss, dark & light, forward & backward, male & female, yin & yang, up & down, hard & soft, in & out, rich & poor ... Tantra is about transcending. Metaphysics is the study of the beyond. It is not an intellectual enterprise but is based on experiment.

Transcending happens through merging. This is the divine art of alchemy. It is the collapse of infinity into a single point. In order to transcend we have to move out of the realm of pairs of opposites. Why do the opposites exist? When 'stillness' and 'dynamism' are about to merge, some 'tension' arises. The stillness is afraid to lose itself into dynamism and the dynamism is afraid to 'lose' itself to stillness. This makes them very alert. So they both rise to a supreme state of consciousness and that is awareness.

It starts, however, with the Witness. We have to leave the field of the ego behind. How do we do that? Can it be done by force? No. We have to be much smarter than that. I have explained to you before the 3-fold strategy. We need to dismantle the personality. It does not go via suppression. Nor is indulgence the way to go, although many people think that that is Tantra. Tantra cannot be learned out of a book. Books become bestsellers by good marketing techniques. Americans are the gurus of marketing. That does not mean that all the American bestselling spiritual authors like X, Y and Z, most of whom I know fairly well, are masters. Let us not misuse those words.

It is hard work. The personality is quite a force and in order to handle it, one needs to be an expert in explosives. One needs to be able to place booby-traps and one needs to be able to dismantle an atomic bomb. Only by thorough and deep inquiry into our real nature AND by practising devotion will buddhi wake up. Buddhi is the higher or most refined intellect. You will need that force to become the witness. It is dormant in most people. Like Kundalini, it lies asleep. A large part of sadhana is to practise this observing. Witnessing is extremely important. And the final truth is that it happens. Or not. But still we advise people to try to practise and to make a supreme effort.

Many human beings are very proud of what they accomplish in the waking state, but for others the waking state is sheer ignorance and people don't have a clue as to how they are totally controlled by outside forces. Nor do they know the consequences of their actions. What a paradox huh?

That is the true meaning of Yoga. For people who are immersed in duality, yoga is a practice. It might happen – by the Grace of God – that suddenly while you are walking the Path, the walker disappears and all that remains is walking. THAT is the merger of stillness and dynamism. That is waking! The ego is left behind like a snake leaves behind his skin, and you move up the tattvas from ego to witness to consciousness to awareness. That is how these rishis know*. The same way that you will come to know. Not by reading. Not by talking but by silence. Silence is the key. Meditation is the way. Dancing is also beautiful. It is very important to exercise the body. To help other people and to live in love and with compassion. Force your intellect to work. Expand it to encompass the multitudes. Trace the multiplicity back to its source. Consciousness is the Source, Course and Goal of life. You are That.

When it is still, there is dynamism and when there is dynamism, there is stillness. But my friends, this is a supreme path. You can have your job and your family. You can be a monk and still make love. And why not? Life is lovely and wonderful. This is the tantric secret to life. How to combine bhoga and yoga? It is difficult. It is not for everybody. It is only for the hero.

Tantra is a noble way of living. It is a supreme philosophy and a highly refined way to live life. To live in an attitude of gratitude. To celebrate life. To be a hero. The one who worships the Goddess. Shakti and Her multiple forms.

The world is diverse. It is multiple. Quantum physics explains that the finest level is particles and waves. Particles disappear into waves and sometimes disappear altogether only to arise again later somewhere else. Later and somewhere else in the time-space continuum. But even this time-space continuum wavers in and out of existence on the verge of a mighty black hole. And we need to become the watcher. This requires deep meditation. Shiva is the Lord of meditation. He meditates for aeons. Totally undisturbed.

Until Shakti lures Him out with her dance. Shakti is moving. She longs to merge with Him.

Most people understand this in the realm of diversity. And you will have to make an effort to start to see the unity that underlies the diversity. The diversity is the great magic show of the divine. And you need to figure out the following question: "What is the matrix?" This leads in to Trika-mysticism.
That will bring you to understand diversity in unity and later on to the experience of unity. Unity is the merging of Shiva and Shakti. The great tantric ritual.

The Tantras are in fact the recording of 'a dialogue' between Lord Shiva and the great Goddess Shakti. This dialogue is filled with allegory and hidden keys. One can only understand it by the aid of the guru who is initiated. This understanding leads to recognition (pratyabhijna). That (the) dialogue is merely Spanda. The Spanda of Shakti. For contracted consciousness, in what we call the impure order, it is the maya; the matrix. So contemplate well THE QUESTION!

* Ages ago they already described principles of quantum physics and astronomy with great detail.

The Light

A friend of mine told me recently that he had seen the light. He thought he was now self-realized and enlightened.

I prefer to say: "The more I see, the more I see there is to see!"

If he had seen the light, what does he see now?

Who is the one who is seeing the light?

Many of these people declare that it is not necessary to meditate anymore. The world is all right with them. They seem to be very happy.

It is not bad to have a modest attitude. In The Path of Yoga, Beauty & Delight we bow a lot. Paul du Marchie made all the doors in his house a bit too low. On purpose, so that we bow every time we go through a door.

Every time...

The light is a huge mystery.

If the light was your face, what would it see if it turned around and looked into a mirror?

Who is the I who has seen the light?

Can the light be separated from the fire?

Can the heat be separated from the light?

Can a spark exist separate from the fire?

Can the smoke exist separate from the spark?

Can the fire exist without the log?

Is the lighting of the match separate from the fire?

Does the sun stop shining when it is night?

Was the light not there before sunrise?

Would you enjoy the moon without the sun?

The moon is always full moon even though we call her half or new moon.

Is the moon ever really half?

Did you ever not see the light?

Would you be able to exist without the light?

Can a TV receive television programs without electricity?

Beauty belongs to The Light.

Seeing, hearing and feeling The Light is beautiful.

Being Delighted is something else!

What is Yoga?

True Yoga is experienced by Grace. It is that Grace we should seek. The shelter of the guru. She who is the remover of ignorance.

Even Shiva needs Shakti. Without Shakti, Shiva is a dead body, inert. Only through Shakti can he recognize his own Divine nature.

Shiva needs the guru in order to realize and to feel the Delight of Pratyabhijna. No guru, no pratyabhijna (recognition). That is why this cult is the Shiva-lineage of Divine Madness. The guru is the one who the river flows through. The river that starts out of the matted hair of Lord Shiva. Mother Ganga. It is that Living Water in which we long to bathe. That holy fire that we worship. The small flame that we adore as the mighty fire.

Without the guru we are lost in the ocean of endless cycles even though we proclaim that we have seen the light.

This is a tradition of mystery. What happens when the whole universe is dissolved? That knowledge is all stored in the Tantras. Yet, it is not knowledge that we are looking for. All 'knowledge' needs to be dispelled. Knowledge means that there still is a knower who walks with a backpack of 'knowledge'. All knowledge is a heavy burden. All knowledge has a knower. Every thought has a thinker. A vira makes the right kind of worship. And that worship is to offer all knowers, thinkers and doers into the mighty, blazing fire until none of them are left and only the Naga remains. That is in fact the start of Tantra.

Tantra is not for beginners. Tantra is for the hero, the noble one. The one who sets out to walk and continues until the walker disappears. Always walking the path; The Path of Yoga, Beauty & Delight.

Real wisdom is in the silence. The ones who are afraid to be silent or to be alone, the ones who go to spiritual parties in order to socialize with others and secretly hope to find their soul mate, they move too much..

The tantrika opens her third eye to witness the inner movement. She watches the galaxy inside. She views the magic show within. She learns how to still the mind instead of letting the tongue wander in Babylonian newsletters and ancient excavations. Eating the dust. Where are you when everything returns to dust?

Shakti is the doorway to Shiva.

Magical moments in our life are birth, orgasm and death. And all the small portals in between. When we go from waking to dreaming. From dreaming to deep sleep. From deep sleep again to waking. The intervals in between our thoughts. A short moment when there is no thinker but just the watcher. There is turya. The Goddess of the three cities. That is the island where this ship is heading. To find the sacred and secret country of Shangri-La. Wrapped in mystery. Only very few ships make it, as the water around the island is governed by mighty storms. Those who like the sun had better go to one of the tropical islands. There are plenty of them.

Is the light stored in the match?

How long can ignorance last?

Can the moon see its own light?

Can you touch the light in the mirror?

How proud is the darkness that is reflected in the mirror?

Is the mirror ever empty?

The mirror doesn't mind the chatter of the matches that It knows are going to die.

The night carries many secrets but she can never win. What is light for an ordinary man, is darkness for the realized.

The mind makes many movements. It makes all movements except the one that would liberate you. Liberate you from the false idea that you need to be liberated. Come, my friend, and drink some more of the wine. Rest your weary head. You've done a lot of ploughing.

The Resistance

The Resistance is very small. They are ordinary people who do remarkable things at night. At night they go diving. They lead a different life. You may know some things that happen on the deck of the ship. But most people don't have a clue what happens when the experienced sailors go diving. It is a whole different way of living and functioning. It is a totally different form of communing and communicating. Under water is a whole different world.

At night, I often watch the stars. Many people do that at night. When people are desperate, hopeless, quiet, in love etc. – all over the world they watch the stars at night. The scene changes so quickly. It is really a magical universe.

We humans are so busy stretching our (outer) limits. Trying to break records. Expanding our boundaries. Fighting over philosophy and religion. We are willing to kill thousands of our brothers because of 'our' ideals, dogmas and our own subjective and highly conditioned sense of morality. Our brain is so underdeveloped in fact. We marvel at the possibilities of our mind. With our mind we give names to the unseen. The mind of man calls Her Allah, Krishna, God or whatever. The Almighty is, however, probably not that impressed by the name we invent for Her.

Look at the stars! We might call this one star Anita, the other Samantha, Ricardo, Sheila and so on, but the stars have been there a long time. Virtually since the beginning. They are the watchers. Human beings can kill each other, invent a new religion, and make life into a fantastic orgy or whatever, the stars just watch. They have seen many things. They are the silent spectators. Like the ocean. The deep blue. We can try to 'conquer' outer space but that doesn't teach us per se anything about the inner space. The infinite inner space is the connecting link.

We have to learn how to dive. Diving is the art of letting go. It has a lot to do with breathing. Pranayama is the science of breathing. In all spiritual traditions there are certain kinds of sacred breathing 'techniques'. They allow you to go into the proper state. Meditation is exactly like diving. You just take the proper angle and let go. That is the key.

So this is what we do in the Resistance. We dive. And teach some others how to dive. You don't have to teach us things about how to live upstairs. That is not our main concern. Those who strive after wealth and material success are very rarely good divers. They have too much to hold on to and are afraid to let go and to step into the unknown. It has been said many times that you will have to jump. When you jump, you can't take too much with you but you should be prepared. 'Prepared' means concentrated and relaxed. The mind is alert and the body is very relaxed.

I took a bath and thought of how many friends do not even have a shower. They only have their tears to comfort each other, and their blood gives meaning to their life. And our concerns over here are where to go to on vacation. Where to get the best Return on Investment. Which clothes shall I wear to the party?

I must honestly tell you that these are not our parties. When you take a red pill and join the Resistance, life changes. There is not much you can do about it. Your life will gain another dimension. You will be mystically initiated. It is almost like you will join an order. However, there are no visible signs in the outer world. We do not wear badges and the like. There is an unspoken sort of hierarchy. You need to be very alert within. The 'right' things will happen in your life. You WILL receive the proper guidance at the right time even when you disagree or wish things to be otherwise. You need to encompass the entire universe and all its aeons of time. There are sacred dimensions in life. Many untold secrets and hidden mysteries. You need to practise how to perceive, sense, intuit and be open to the voices and messages from the Beyond. The most important thing is to be very patient.

Life in the Resistance – for a diver – is very different. During the day – like Neo – we do our ordinary jobs. No problem. We take care of our family, friends and responsibilities. ENJOY life but don't waste your time! There are ways to sit around the campfire. Allow yourself to be stretched. ALWAYS BE TRUE TO YOURSELF! Find out very thoroughly what that means.

And follow the directions of the saints, sages and other 'ranking officers' (see The Matrix). Be very aware of what you ask of life. Know very well what you are willing to give! It is easy to make proper choices when all is going well, but how will you react in adversity. When they try to imprison a friend? Where is your common sense at that moment? Will you be able to act out of wisdom? Then you have to set out for wisdom (NOW).

Who are the wise ones on the planet? Are they the role models that you read about in newspapers, magazines and that you hear about on radio and see on television? Do you meet them at the seminars and parties? So figure out very well what you are heading for and what you need to do. Can you listen to the birds? Hear the wind whisper to you? Allow her to caress you? Can you accept the love in the mysterious ways that it comes to you instead of holding on to your ideas of how things should be? Always be ready to help other people, but know very well who your friends are. You become a bit like the people you tend to 'socialize' with a lot. Some people even start to look like the pigs that they eat. They talk horseshit, and don't get me wrong. Horses are very noble animals. But only by themselves or with a noble warrior or Goddess riding them. Be grateful that you can learn how to ride (surf / dive) instead of slapping yourself for wasting so much of your time already.

So be that noble warrior and the Goddess of Mercy and jump on those horses. Head up to the Sky! Sit steady in the saddle and be ready to offer a flower. Be ready to draw the sword. Be ready to die and even to give away your robe. Know very well whether you want to live on the surface of life or whether you want to join the underground Resistance. There is not much we can promise you. We are only setting out for the Truth.

But when you firmly decide to join the Resistance, it is a life long promise. It is a way of life and you need to be willing to make some sacrifices. Maybe even some large ones. Nobody is forcing you. You can join when you are ready, and move deeper and closer when you feel you are ready or thirsty for 'the next'. NEVER GO TOO FAST! The downfall might be large... It will all become very clear in due course. The code of the Resistance is very clear. There is nothing that I need to tell you about how it works. It is all up to you!

There are no medals to be earned! Sorry...

Nataraj on 'Control'

Control is an intriguing word. We should differentiate between 'control', 'self control' and 'mastery'. Control is a function of the ego. I want to control my life, my wife etc. Self-control can be acquired by a human being and is necessary to slay the animal inside all of us. It brings out the higher mind. Mastery is something else.

So control is a function of the ego,
Self-control is a function of the (higher) mind, while
Mastery is a function of soul / Spirit.

This signifies our journey from clinging to the known, which is false, to the real, which is the embracing of the unknown and the great mystery of life. Mastery is only available to those who first learn some self-control. In the Path of Yoga, Beauty & Delight it is not only a question of austerity. Shiva indeed signifies self-control. Nataraj however is the great Cosmic Dancer. Here is the divine paradox. We combine yoga and bhoga. Most westerners are, however, very well acquainted with bhoga (pleasure). Their sadhana will be more directed towards inquiry and meditation in order to learn to still the mind and to develop some self-control. This is necessary to awaken buddhi. 'Buddhi' is the higher intellectual centre and is connected with the higher emotional centre, which is necessary to arouse the Heart. Our experience of pleasure greatly changes upon expansion of consciousness.

In our tantric academy, the real practice of tantric lovemaking with initiations starts on the fourth floor. Tantra is for the vira, the noble person or the hero. First, one needs to go through strong personal development. Everything that has been repressed needs to be brought out. Not to indulge and not to suppress. Most people have strong issues to work through with regard to sexuality and the feminine and the masculine. This happens on the first and second floor. The third floor (stage) is for the start of gnosis and initiations into the secret doctrine. Here we really discover what it is to be a man and what it is to be a woman.

When certain qualities have been developed like patience, compassion, (universal) love, and tolerance, and there is a fertile ground for continued training in Tantra philosophy, the door to the fourth floor is open. When is one ready for that space? When one is settled in Yoga. When the mind is settled down. When many impurities have been worked through. The main thing is that the attachment to bhoga is broken. Bhoga is fine. The world is beautiful. But a dirty mind makes it dirty. Tantra is more than just a gem. What we have to present is the Kohinoor of the East, the Kohinoor of spirituality and Tantra.

This Kohinoor will immediately kill someone who is not ready. We need to get adjusted to the light bit by bit. That is why this Path of Yoga, Beauty & Delight is actually a cover up for Yoga, Beauty & The Light. So, my friends, I advise you again to take on a serious spiritual practice. Many are still drowning in all sorts of spiritual ideas and concepts. I am not interested in your models at all. You need to learn how to drink. There are other ships and you are most welcome to find your way to another ship with a captain that you like better because he is not a control freak. Or because he is more kind to people. Or he encourages people more. This is a Shiva-cult with a strong adoration for the Goddess. It is really not for everybody. You are cordially invited to shop around. But it is very difficult for me to work with people who are hammered at by all sorts of blacksmiths. I have a rather unique way of welding. I weld with very hot fire. I forge several metals into each other. Everything needs to be done in a proper way.

If you have your own ideas about how to weld, how to do it, what is needed and when you are ready, you are most welcome to do it that way. This is very precise alchemy. We are talking about the transition of ordinary consciousness, which is a dark black pool, to higher states of consciousness. It is a process of Divine Madness because you need to go out of your mind. Some of you are doing well. Others are really not grasping at all what is happening because you are strongly holding on to ideas of the past and have no eye to clearly see, feel and sense the present situation. It is a mystic journey and the mind cannot fathom what is happening in the other dimension of life.

Human beings have become weak. They eat food out of cans. Watch TV. Move around in cars. Our environment is polluted with over 70,000 chemicals. You have to be very steady and an active mind is never steady. It needs to be thoroughly inquired into. Instead of talking, it would be better to ask intelligent questions or to be silent. Do the work! Don't be proud or arrogant. Slay all feelings of superiority.

It is easy to load up with things. Becoming empty is a totally different process. When you are anchored to a master, you influence your master in a certain way, even when his body is on another continent. That is why a master is very careful about whom he takes on board. Fraudulent students can cause problems in the future. That is why I say that this is a team-effort. You should do all you can to help each other. If you want to master Yoga, Beauty & Delight, focus solely on that. It is difficult enough. Like with a computer, you need to do a virus check every now and then. Not only on yourself but check and clean the whole system.

Relationships...

All of us are experts in them and yet none of us are.

This is maybe the most difficult subject of all. Shrouded in rules and expectations.

The mysterious play of the object, the subject and the process of relating.

Sometimes these three are so close and yet they are often so far away.

The play of hide-and-seek.

Even great divers have big challenges in relationships.

Even best selling authors on this subject are more than ever bewildered by the unpredictability of the human heart, mind and soul.

It is clear that when two people relate and there is a lot of unprocessed stuff in their subconscious mind, all that 'stuff' is going to be acted out in the relationship. Not in the beginning. In the beginning all is fine. But when they get to know each other better.... Both bring in the pain from their upbringing, and maybe from other unresolved relationships and possible karma.. We all have had our pain and hardships to endure. Where does it go?

Whole books can be written about this subject. How is it from the viewpoint of The Path of Yoga, Beauty & Delight?

Foremost is the importance of being alone.

Human interactions are very important and precious. It is a great way to test us. How is our dominance? How is our letting go? How is our acceptance? How is our self-esteem? Where is our pride? How possessive are we? How is our care? How deep is our love? What about our need to retaliate? Can we be more humble?

In our School there are many possibilities:
Some people are single
Others are in a tight relationship
Some prefer 'free relationships'
Others live a celibate life

The celibate life can be lived in a very social way or it can be more reclusive and monastic. Many tantric practitioners and masters live a celibate life. They usually don't have that many relationship challenges. So this is a serious and good option. However: not as an escape Celibacy should come with maturity.

The concept of 'free relationships' (Osho-style) sounds interesting to many. But be very careful. As Paul du Marchie said, it is possible but it should be a piece of art. Not messing around. It is certainly not a game or a contest. It has to be done with honesty, openness and in a respectful way. All the while one has to practise self-inquiry.

Being loyal and devoted to one particular person is a beautiful thing as long as it is beautiful. Often it becomes ugly. It all depends on our shadow: the animal. What is our level of mastery and of ripeness? How responsible are we? What is our capacity to sacrifice? Can we be detached and at the same time properly involved?

In classical Indian philosophy there are several stages that I describe in my book Shiva. We must, however, acknowledge that times have drastically changed. In our school we will see a rise in monastic life. Our monastic life will however be modernized. We can live a monastic life while living in the world. It is obvious that the matrix is getting overheated. Politicians are going insane. Religious leaders are losing their religion. Corruption is running at high tide. People will want to turn away from the system. There is so much concentrated wealth in the West that it makes us sick.

So many of us have such pure longings in our heart and soul. We long for peace, love and brotherhood of man. For many of us it is hard to live in this world of cruelty, grossness, war, hate, conflict, jealousy, ignorance, male dominion, suppression, arrogance, misplaced superiority, blindness, selfishness, sexual abuse etc. It is only logical that we want to create our own place. A place of sanity. Many people want to return to a simpler life. They would be welcome in our ashram.

We may have been very ambitious in our life but when we see the violence around us and inside... Many people experience the internal violence of cancer cells. There are many viruses going around. The state of the average human being is not well at all. It is characterized by a restless mind, a disturbed personality with many disorders, a sick and weak body, very little self-knowledge and lots of ignorance.

How can such a naïve character ever be happy in relationships? It looks for the source of happiness in a cupboard where it cannot be found. It looks only externally. It puts on new make-up, wears the latest fashion, goes to a seminar on positive thinking, learns flirting techniques, tries some pills and this and that but everything fades away. Nothing is lasting.

Present-day spirituality is very confusing. Many people who live a very simple life and whom we never hear of are much more advanced than many of the popular lecturers and authors. It is a totally absurd idea for us to learn spirituality from the masters of marketing. They are the ones who didn't like the idea that they couldn't make money out of Jesus Christ and therefore they invented Santa Claus and the habit of buying expensive presents.

Hell is not a place out there and neither is heaven. They are internal states and I guess many of you understand what the difference is. You have been tormented by the mind and also experienced the peaceful silence.

We will be much happier and more fulfilled in our relationships when we work through the shadow and learn what it means to be responsible. This is very difficult.

Energy

We can say that everything is, in a certain way, energy. Everything is a different vibration of the same energy. Sound is vibration. But even matter is energy in motion. Also emotions are energy in motion (E-motion). Anger is a different frequency from patience. The essence of matter is non-matter. All matter is a vacuum with a particle moving around in it at lightning speed, fading in and out of existence, sometimes as a wave and sometimes seemingly appearing as a particle. Even our bodies are a void. And our mind exists in this void and energy field, turning nothing into some-thing. Catching all sorts of thought-waves and making them real by identification. This way, we live in a world of duality. We feel that there is a mystery in and behind all of this but it is not easy to tear the walls away. The matrix world looks, sounds and feels very real. The matrix is real. It does exist but it is not the only 'reality'. There is a whole lot more going on. This 'whole lot more' is unperceivable to the gross senses.

Somewhere we sense and know that there is more, but this is incomprehensible to the mind. We need to stop relying on our mind. But our mind is very dominant. How to not rely on our mind? This is the big question in Eastern philosophy. Most answer that the key is detachment and renunciation. We might be unable to tear the walls away because of false identification.

In this ocean, some parts are very quiet and in other parts there are wild waves and raging storms. We must be able to survive any kind of weather, but for deep contemplation it is easier to start practising when the sea is quiet. That is the best way to learn how to dive, but once we learn how to dive we can even do it amidst stormy weather (strong and unpredictable moves in the matrix). As soon as you dive beneath the waves, you are out of the influence of the weather.

Under water there are different 'rules' from above. It is a whole different scene.

Where and how to find the smooth waters in our turbulent lives to start and to accelerate our 'diving-career'?

We have to learn to settle down the mind. Meditating in a cave or close to a waterfall is different from meditating on an airplane. A wooden house carries a different energy to an air-conditioned modern office building. On an empty stomach is better than just after a heavy meal. In a peaceful environment it is different to being surrounded by a group of hostile extremists. Meditation in cool weather is different from meditating in the burning sun.

Tantriks even take into consideration (it all has a different meaning / energy):
- Wearing long hair or being bald
- When to shave or cut hair
- Wearing cotton or silk
- Wearing different coloured clothes
- To cover the head or not
- To drink out of a glass cup or a brass cup
- At what time to meditate
- How to dispose of flowers used in rituals
- The effect of certain days of the week
- Certain things should not touch the floor
- Certain tantric tools must never be touched by others
- Certain things are to be kept absolutely secret and confidential

This list could go on for MUCH longer and there are many details to share later. For now, it is enough to understand that we are influenced by each other's energy. There are certain influences from the past and the future and strong influences from the moon, the sun and other planets / constellations. There is no doubt about it even though we still need to explain how ultimately there is no causation.

The most important thing from a guru may not be his or her words or directions, but simply being in his or her energy-field. Unplugging is not a matter of words at all. We have to train our subtle senses. We have to learn to use our finer antennae. This is entering the mystical domain. This is how Harry Potter found platform 9 3/4.

When we function in the gross domain all the time, it is hard to find the door opening. The guru can show us the door-entrance but we need to be receptive. For most people, the matrix-world is of primary importance and they are interested in some spiritual growth on the side. There is however no some-thing to be achieved. It is all or No-thing. The true disciple will experience the subtle workings of the guru-principle inside. Borders are fading. An inner strength is rising. Mystery is dawning. There is less clinging to the known and principles of certainty. That means that amidst the highest uncertainty true knowledge is dawning. The guru is the one who creates this uncertainty. The joy of living dangerously! Dangerously means letting go and not clinging to the known.

The known is a frozen picture. The unknown is a dazzling moving experience. The experience of infinity in a tiny point. The unknown is Love. Ordinary 'love' is just an illusion of possession. Love cannot possess or be possessed. Only an ego likes to chain things down, while unnoticed he chains himself down. Only love can love and be loved. That energy is one. Real love happens when we step out of the way and allow Life to happen. When the mind is not there to interfere with thoughts about love. Love is an ocean. That ocean condenses like a wave. Another wave is sending you this text through the ocean. The ocean is the white light that links these letters and passes through your eyes to stimulate a brain cell, which is wired to the blood pulsating in your heart. That movement in your heart is the ocean stirring you to wake up.

You were so identified with all the misery of the wave and had not yet discovered how you were holding on to the prison of the known. You were identifying too much. That costs much energy and is tiring. By letting go I start to flow. When I flow I can dive. When I dive I experience that there is much Beauty & Delight. My sense of 'i' melts away as salt in the water. All that remains is the 'I am'. The energy behind the energy. The light of the light (and darkness). The stillness of the breeze. The breeze that makes the tree leaves float through the air without any patterns. Circling around the pillars of the temple. The pillars, which stand alone but carry the same roof. The roof of the sky. But you are the horizon!

Individual Effort

The world is full of paradoxes.

Physicists try to unravel the mystery of the universe. They can, however, only measure the matrix. What do they know about parallel universes? Philosophers have their laws of deduction and logic. How can we understand the workings of the entire universe? It is a sheer impossibility when clinging on to the mind. And very few people have the audacity to renounce the world, and therewith their mind

We want to know. That is only logical. And in wanting to know we have to learn to accept mystery. It is only in and through the mystery that we come to full understanding and blossoming.
It is heroic that we try. We do sadhana. We pray. Meditate. Try this system and that philosophy. Every faith and religion seems to catch a glimpse of a deeper reality. We have to inquire however, into 'the person' who is seeking to know. What are the motives for liberation or realization? Maybe it is not for us to come to know something. We have to be very careful in using certain words. We can make quite a lot of progress in the spiritual arena but for the ultimate step we need to let go.

God can make Him or Herself known to us but it is not up to us to find or discover Him or Her. We can only disappear. This disappearance is called surrender. That is why we talk about a love affair with the Beloved. Sometimes She makes Herself known and at other times She seemingly disappears and all we are left with is a sweet memory with a tingling sensation.

Hafiz wrote that even the voice of a man who curses God because of an empty tyre, is music to the ears of a mystic. Simply hearing the holy name makes Hafiz go into ecstasy. And he still calls himself an old pilgrim... Every interaction in creation is, for him, divine. It is an opportunity to dive in (divine → div [in] e). Hafiz continuously describes beautiful experiences of the state that we call multi-dimensional awareness. He permanently lives in Divine Madness.

Science calls religion irrational and religion calls scientists irrational. So let's be irrational. What is the fun of rationality anyway? It is nothing more than the prison of the known. We have to dive into the unknown and allow it to sweep us away while accepting all consequences. The joy of living dangerously. The mystical life is unpredictable. The future is not known. Not known to men. Maybe everything is predestined. Nobody has ever predicted everything. Even those who know how everything works do not necessarily have accurate foreknowledge. You reading this page is perhaps Shiva's Grace. All happens by the Grace of the Lord. That is surrender. It does not mean that we sit back and relax. That is a gross misunderstanding.

Of course, you can sit back and relax in the matrix. There are forces at hand. It is not a particularly bright moment in the history of mankind. The mind in awe at the possibilities of science, and strongly chained by the darkness of fundamentalist religion, is slaughtering his brothers and sisters and causing incredible harm and suffering. Very painful suffering.
The nervous system of human beings is the peak of evolution and it comes with a choice. It is

possible to sacrifice our (individual) selves and to be jolted with divine energy so that the source and the goal collapse and we are present to witness the great event. It is also possible that instead of sacrificing our own individual nature we kill the divine each and every moment because we go back to sleep every second. Waking is so enjoyable!

Tantra philosophy stems from the same time as the great civilization of the Egyptians. The Egyptians worshipped the sun. They called it RA. They also worshipped the great Nile, just as in India they worship Mother Ganga, the giver of Life. Without the Nile, Egypt would just be a place of sand. The Nile is 6,000 kilometres long. The same as some other rivers on the planet. Imagine the long locks of hair. They usually worship the sun with fire and gold. We can train our finer sense in order to really see. But when we really see, we are being seen. And the Self curves back on itself. That is the meaning of the Sanskrit word 'namah'. Curving back on Itself again and again.

The second of the Wisdom Goddesses is Tara. There are ten Mahavidyas, as you know. Maha of course means great, as we all know, and Vidya means knowledge or wisdom. It is a supreme wisdom, the wisdom of the Self. It is not objective wisdom. Objective wisdom requires a knower who knows something else by the process of knowing. The Self however cannot be known like that.

There is nothing to write about the Self. We can only point and explain what it is not and even that is incorrect. For pure knowledge, the 'knower' must die. The knower has many thinkers. Every thought has its own 'thinker'. The Self is the Witness and beyond. Even quantum physics has now come to investigate consciousness itself. Mystics also dwell in that 'region'. Divers love the place for excellent diving. Great captains always steer their ship in that direction. It is always a tough sailing trip. It is easier to sing about Her than to try to explain. While dancing we come closer than discussing that which cannot be discussed. In all the great civilizations also the intellect peaked. They were very religious people. Their art was superior. They were very civilized which is why we call them great civilizations. But what characterizes a great civilization? I have not looked it up in the book but let's discuss. What would you say?

I'd say:
There is justice and order. All sorts of arts are very well developed. Great development of science. And especially, there is a religious system of great depth. That does not mean organization, dogma or fundamentalism but it means highly esoteric understanding. They usually also had profound rituals with fire, gold etc. This high esoteric understanding was expressed as the merging of the male and the female. High respect for and expression of both!

That was the same in the Vedic civilization. It is remarkable how the Vedic civilization resembled the Egyptians. In the times of Raj Ram, there was supreme justice and order in the Vedic civilization. It is all documented in the Vedas. They are the oldest writings of mankind (according to many...). And my friends, here comes the shocking news: If a civilization is very advanced, if it is most advanced – most also meaning more advanced than other systems or civilizations – it should also know something about the past and the future and be able to protect itself so as not to get lost. Most ancient civilizations peaked and they were lost.

Nobody can exactly re-construct the Egyptian civilization. We know many things about it. But nobody is 100% certain how the pyramids were built. With our mind we can only imagine that they were built with manual labour. But if that is the case we should be more in awe than we presently are. These huge blocks came from many, many miles away and were cut with razor-sharp precision. They lie so precisely that you cannot even slip a razor blade in between! That is indeed a great work of art. It is greater than great. And still it got lost. Some people may have had a previous life in Egypt. Virtually everybody who does a past life reading hears that he or she has been an Egyptian priest. Well, maybe there just were many priests in Egypt, because there were also many priestesses!

But still, nobody has a perfect recollection. This is the speciality of the tantric tradition. They have a perfect recollection. It is a matter of sruti and smriti. This is the science and art of forgetting and remembering. The big question, as I wrote previously, is what to remember and what (when?) to forget? The tantriks are great masters. You'd be surprised at their capabilities. You can read about it in books like 'Masters of the far East' part I and II by Baird T. Spalding. These books describe awesome and great siddhis. But, unfortunately, not the most interesting ones.

These things nobody can acquire by themselves. Spirituality in the East has always been a matter of master and disciple for obvious reasons. Some things can only be given. Very rarely were the great civilizations a democracy. Very rarely. I think never. The ultimate 'ruler' was always a priest. Or a God-man, or, of course and maybe most superior, a God-woman. A pharaoh. The great priestess: Mahadevi. Mahadevi is the wife of Lord Shiva. She has ten forms in which she can manifest Herself. This is known as the hidden knowledge of the ten Mahavidyas.

The knowledge (this power and these mysteries) is very well protected. Very well. In a typical tantric manner. The knowledge is surrounded by perversity. Some of these Goddesses are very ugly, nasty or aggressive. There are vivid acts of sexuality in it where Chinnamaste is riding on Shiva (or in another narration on the copulating bodies of Goddess Rati and her husband Kama (God of Love)) who lies like a dead corpse. This is in fact an asana. Asana means 'posture'. It is an external posture with a certain breathing and inner exercise. The power of the Goddesses is put into a mantra. The essence can only be gained through a mantra. We can look at pictures of the Goddesses, but that is not where their essence is.

These mantras need to be recited often. So often that at a certain moment the practitioner is gone. That is the way to gain the power of the mantra and a boon of the Goddess. She is the deity of a certain yantra. A yantra is an esoteric, geometric form. The great pyramid is a three-dimensional yantra called a Meru. Meru is also a mountain in the Himalayas. The pyramids are positioned in an exact geometric grid. They are very precisely positioned against a certain astral constellation. In my meditation room I used to perform rituals in front of an empowered yantra from Durga. It was given to a great tantric master during his abhishek and he passed it on to me a couple of months later with precise instructions for worship. An abhishek is a ritual in which certain siddhis and/or initiations are given to a tantric practitioner or a master. It is like a powerful diksha or initiation.

Without these initiations not much progress can be made in the tantric field. During the diksha the master gives a mantra to the vira (worthy disciple). This mantra is not just a word; it is a symbol that carries the Essence. That is the power of these masters. I have written that this is their speciality and why Tantra has never been lost for thousands of centuries. It was a very precise lineage whereby the Essence always poured like a river from master to disciple. And all this under strict protocol.

So even the mantra of the Goddess has to be charged with the energy of the master. And then, after strict adherence, after a while maybe and maybe not the Goddess offers Her boon. This is the tradition of Tantra. But now listen closely to what I say about how these masters work because it is not like anything you can imagine. They are very intelligent people who act like complete fools. That is what makes them mystics. They become drunk, so to speak, because of diving in and out. If you see the movie 'Le Grand Bleu' you'll see exactly what I mean.

In most of the religions, there are certain objects that are considered to be holy like a stone or a hair of the prophet/Buddha. Any science or system uses tools. Tantra also has many tools. Let me tell you about one of these tools and you can link it to why I said that an ashram is of utmost importance. In Tantra there are also certain tools that have imbibed sacred energy.

For a master there is one thing that is most important. The movie The Matrix explains this very clearly and precisely. I am talking about finding the worthwhile disciple. This is very difficult. A master only imparts his essence to the worthy disciple. This essence is via the Shaktipata. That is the mystery that is employed in Tantra philosophy. It typically belongs to non-dual Kashmir Saivism. Some other systems talk about it, but it is the great science, art and philosophy of non-dual Kashmir Saivism where the principle of Shaktipata (Anugraha; Divine Grace) is exactly described. We even describe 27 and 36 levels of intensity of Grace with different names.

It is a disaster for a master and almost a curse for him if he or she cannot find the worthwhile disciple. This is the truth and you can read about the exact protocol in the scripts of Kashmir Saivism. The only thing that I can say as a disciple of my master is that it does not go as I thought it would. And that is of course very logical. Some masters did not have a master of their own. They gained everything by recollection. All the esoteric knowledge of colours, 'empowerments', chakras, auras, kundalini, the tarot, astrology, the kabbalah, rituals for lovemaking and many other things came to them just by inner recollection. In the vedantic setting we call this 'cognizing'. A rishi (seer as in maharishi) can cognize the Vedas. That means that he cognizes deeper hidden truths placed in his awareness. He looks within. Many of these masters do not and have not read books although they do often write.

My first master Maharishi Mahesh Yogi often said: "Knowledge of the book stays in the book!" His master Swami Brahmamanda Saravati was also initiated in Sri Vidya. His function of Shankaracharya in Jyotir Math was very auspicious. Jyotir Math is a very holy town in the Himalayas. A small village in fact. Very small. I was there. A Shankaracharya is a keeper of the flame. A keeper of the wisdom. They often worship the Divine Mother. Others say that that is just some ritual stuff. Let them say whatever they want to say.

I have explained to you that in all the great civilizations they practised rituals. And not because they were stupid. We cannot say that the Egyptians were stupid. Christians want us to believe that the Egyptians were cruel slave drivers but that is false. There is just a lot of bullshit going around in religious circles. I just wonder why all these religions are still so popular. Their results are not that impressive. I heard that people in the west are interested in a good return on investment. I personally wonder why all these smart investors are still so religiously fundamentalist. Why don't they ease up a bit and study what they have accomplished in spiritual and religious terms. There are just too many empty buildings and a lot of wars. Mostly religious wars.

Unequal wars. Uncivilized wars. Cruel wars. That is slavery. Walking on the battlefield, feeling like a superior hero who is risking his life for *a good cause*. And what is the good cause?

WHAT IS THE GOOD CAUSE?

Fighting terrorism? *$#@* !?

Don't tell me they all do it for that reason?

All this war and terrorism in order to fight terrorism? Is that what all these people are dying for and are being suppressed for? In that case, I do not vote for this as being a great civilization. I am sorry. It is still slavery. A great civilization has to do with awareness. There is some nobility. There is showering of wisdom. The female is always greatly respected. That is not the case in our time.

I invite the great Goddess. I invoke Her presence amongst us. May she guide and bless our journey. Let wisdom rule. I don't care whether I am rich or poor but at least give me the wisdom to accept my circumstances and give me the strength to help my fellow beings that are suffering. Let our lives be about that. Let us build an ashram where that spirit can rise in us all. So that we find the strength to surrender our life in order to witness the building of great pieces of art. The weaving of a Magic Carpet.

Let us play the flute in a hypnotizing way to invite people to come in and then unnoticeably cut off their heads with a razor-sharp sword. Let the blood flow as the wisdom Goddesses usually like blood. You will come to understand later on why, in their pictures, they often carry a sword with which they cut off heads. Chinnamaste even cuts off her own head. Out of her neck come two streams of blood. This signifies Ida and Pingala, the two life-giving channels that merge into the all-powerful Sushumna, which rises to the 1,000-petalled lotus of the Brahmanandhra. This is where Shiva and Shakti make love.

All the esoteric secrets of non-dual Kashmir Saivism are about the Sushumna and the tiny little opening. The blue pearl.

Sometimes it happened that a master could not find a worthy disciple even though many thousands adored him. He would then, close to the time of his death, put all of his powers into several objects. These objects he would bury or hide very well. Then, much later – often many centuries later – a passer-by would feel drawn towards a certain cave or a tree. He 'had to' pick up that stone. And then something happened. The transmission happened instantaneously. There was nothing he could do about it. That does not mean that it all came to awareness right away. It could take quite a while and depended on certain things.

For a tantric master, it is important to be surrounded by Shakti-energy. Certain things are more conducive to that. Society usually cannot stand a tantric master being surrounded by many women.

So that is how these tantric tools work. Tantra is all about emissions of certain energy. When a tantric master transmits certain powerful energy to a tree, the tree will immediately shrink. A great tantric master is known to have drunk a bottle of hydrochloric acid. A whole bottle! He recycled it through his body and peed it out early the next morning after the Sri Chakra ritual.

There are many things to explore in the right setting.

In-depth Study

Before we start an in-depth study of Tantra, we really have to clean up and straighten out our lives. This is tougher than most people imagine.

- It means you develop objectivity in thinking.
- It means you develop good health.
- It means you first become strong and assertive and then you surrender. Surrendering is an act of courage and of wisdom, not of weakness or desperation!
- It means you don't allow yourself to be bribed, manipulated or suppressed unless you consciously choose to.
- It means you'll have to learn to make tough decisions and to let go of things out of the past that don't support the jewel that you are.
- It means you don't allow memories to (mis)use you, but that you learn to manage them. Use your memories like a dictionary.
- It means you don't gossip, hide away or use excuses. You will have to learn what responsibility is.
- It means you learn to forgive and to accept. In no way is a complaining attitude acceptable! It also means that you don't make a mess of your relationships (for most people this assignment is enough for the rest of their lives!).
- Don't lose yourself in sentiments while maintaining an open heart.
- It does not mean that you develop a therapeutic relationship with everybody. It does mean that you make a superhuman effort to see through all your projections and come to grips with the tricks of your mind.

You see... the point is, that life is. It is as it is and because it is as it is, it is good. It is perfect. Not perfect for the mind maybe, but that is the problem of and for the mind.

No need to fight against what is. Yet we will have to learn how to fight. You will have to stand up for yourself and others. If you have a family and a burglar comes in, shoots your wife and points his gun at one of your children, you shouldn't sing a mantra that all is 'fine and perfect'. I promise you that you won't. It is best to stay calm and make a joke. Do something very surprising. And then defend your family. If the Nazis invade our country and do a lot of harm, you should go into the resistance. It is (y)our task to uphold dharma (right action). For that we give away our life. At least, we are willing to. You also have to know something about the art of war.

What I write seems to be very contradictory to many people. It is actually a very subtle and thin line. In a previous mail, I wrote that you shouldn't strive for wealth yet it is OK to be wealthy if it happens that way. Wealth should not come by ambition. You do strive to fulfil your duties and to do your work as well as you can, which is with attention and awareness. You make everything divine. You offer it to your master or higher Self. You forget yourself and remember the Self. It is all a matter of forgetting and remembering (sruti and smriti). Don't go into nihilism.

Thinking versus Drinking and the Art of War

Many people have some ideas what Tantra is about. Virtually nobody has a clue what non-dual Kashmir Saivism entails. Even the Path of Yoga, Beauty & Delight is still more or less a mystery. It has to do with becoming hot & wet. For now understand it to be refinement.

Tantra can be a study for the mind. Usually this is so for the people who write books on Tantra. Really it is about surrender and devotion. Surrender and devotion are qualities of the heart. The mind can never understand the depth of Tantra. The mind is incapable of fully knowing.

Philosophers talk about their understanding. Whether reality is dual or non-dual. Whether it is like *this* or *that*. But Ultimate Reality always transcends any and all words, understanding and interpretations. Hopefully we are not heading to become another –ism. Right now using

words is virtually inescapable. I foresee a time in the future when we will use very few or maybe even no words at all.
That however is only possible when people become very ripe for the true experience of Tantra. It will be a silent communion. It is a very high level of refinement where we can commune without using words. This merger happens through devotion. Lots of things still have to be burnt.

In Tantra-philosophy we distinguish several 'types' of disciples. I spoke about the vira. The vira however is not the highest. A divya is much more sattvic than even a vira. Sattvic meaning more pure. It is difficult to maintain that innocence and purity in this society. Maybe, and in fact I suspect that, some of you viras will have children who are divyas. Ashrams are not only for us, but also even more for them. To prepare the way.

An ashram is often described as a washing-machine; in a washing machine you throw in dirty clothes and they come out clean. Nobody knows where the dirt went, but it is gone. It is the same for an ashram. It takes in tamasic tendencies and they are miraculously transformed into sattva/purity.
A tantrik often challenges/transcends the norms that society has put around purity and impurity. Which norms could be the ones for us (to challenge?) in the west in the year 2002?

Tantra is the sadhana by which Shakti awakens in the Muladhara and rises to meet and merge with Shiva in the lotus-flower of Brahmamandhra. By this merger wine spontaneously starts to drip from our head (the Sahasrara) down. This wine is indeed the consciousness full of bliss. Self-referral consciousness. This is the bliss of ananda. Ordinary wine gives a temporal pleasure. It is an ego-sensation (sensory-based). The wine of Sat-Chit-Ananda is non-local.

The people who learned to drink this wine are even amidst pain and pleasure, success and failure, praise and criticism. They are less affected by temporal changes and know that even resistance and acceptance belong to the personality. The personality needs to be polished. We need some hammering to come to the deeper and more profound insight that is radical. One cannot pretend to take a red pill and keep on negotiating, fighting and flighting. There are no compromises possible with a red pill. The Truth can only be experienced when the mind is totally still.

It takes a lot of refinement to be able to experience the river of wine inside. It will only happen by and through devotion. It is not by force. It is not because of 'power'. In fact 'you' have nothing to do with it. It is such a delight. The guru can work on our tamasic tendencies but only when there is strong devotion. Otherwise the job at hand is simply too dangerous.

The old-style was for people to practise heavy ascetism and to renounce the world. The Path of Yoga, Beauty & Delight requires the same discipline and will power, and now we also include the world and some of the sense-pleasures that it offers. It is the most sublime understanding and path where we combine yoga (unity) and bhoga (pleasure). It is the approach that the world is drastically looking for. It is the most modern form of spirituality that you can imagine, while it is also very authentic.

You must also understand why I so often explain that it is not for everyone. Kundalini is a mighty force and the nervous system needs to be well prepared. This preparation is not through reading and listening to words, but it requires a strict sadhana.

Start with the refinement, my friends. Refinement brings fine wine. Don't whine but tune in. Make yourself strong. Tantra is not for sheep. A disciple is a lion. Neo was certainly not a nerd or a cowherd. But tune in. It took Neo quite a while to figure out how Morpheus had been trying to contact him for along time already. Knock ... knock ... Refine your senses and antennae.

I, however still/also have some preferences. I like good wine. Also, I do not deem it necessary that people who tread the Path of Yoga, Beauty & Delight feel that it is important to travel to India, Nepal or Tibet. Find the inner Himalayas! Also, I don't see the need for us to wear Indian clothes. Many austere tantric practices, like those on a cremation ground etc., are also not relevant for us. I desire our approach to be authentic AND adapted to modern times and the west. Any 'approach' will be called an –ism but what characterises an –ism is fundamentalism and lack of Living Water. No wonder Hafiz often speaks about wine. In his circles (Islam) wine was strictly forbidden! And *wine* is the word that hints at the sweet ambrosia of Life: this kind of wine is truly Living Water!

No wonder virtually all ancient cultures worship the river. The river; the life-giving force. Even many gospel-songs praise the river. Any river is in itself a mystery. It starts out with some drops. A small brook arises. Some other brooks join and a river comes into existence. A mighty river connecting civilisations. A means for transport. Finally any river merges into the ocean. By the heat of the sun water vaporises and becomes a cloud. Human beings are a heavily pregnant cloud trying to stay up high, but bound to drop its load. No cloud lasts forever. When the rain pours down on the earth some of it becomes a brook again. This is the eternal flow of life.

Wherever two merge into one, that is a holy spot for tantriks. Our body has many nadis (channels of subtle energy). These nadis are unnoticeable to the eye. They are in the astral realm. Where several nadis cross, we call it a *marma-point*. In ayurveda they massage these points. When even more important nadis cross, it is a chakra. In the third eye (in between and slightly above the eye brows) the two most famous nadis *Ida* and *Pingala* merge into Sushumna. Ida and Pingala are the lunar and solar channels of energy. Sushumna is the mighty river! A tantric yogi seeks this passage into Sushumna. It is very difficult.

A river washes us clean. It washes away garbage and ignorance.
'No man can step into the same river twice.'
That is why we speak of Living Water.
The divine is indeed everywhere. It is however not enough to mentally apprehend this. It must be fully and consciously realised by the aspirant. That is the true delight. And that is the reason we call this path The Path of Yoga, Beauty & Delight.

Aum Shanti
Aum Shanti
Aum Shanti

I pray that by the Grace of the Guru and Lord Shiva all these words become a Living Reality for the true devotees.

On 'The Force'

Yesterday, I watched Star Wars, Episode I: the Phantom Menace. They speak about The Force and clarify a bit what this mysterious force is. It lives in everybody and all living beings and insentient things. In some people it is stronger than in others. Some people can hear it better and feel it better than others. They go more with the Force. Their understanding of the Force is more refined. They trust the Force. They seek to listen to the Force. They dare to let their lives be guided by the Force.

This sounds very much like what we call Shakti.

Shakti is everywhere and in everyone. In some it is more dormant and in others it is more alive. It is not up to us to investigate why this is so. It just is. Tantra philosophy says that by strong sadhana and under the guidance of the guru, it is possible that Shakti will become stronger. This is the awakening of Ma Kundalini. We can talk and write about what kundalini is, but it has to be experienced. Nobody can sufficiently explain it to you in advance.

In most people, kundalini is dormant. There is no difference between kundalini and Shakti. The guru is able to ignite a small flame in a devotee. It is however a very precarious process. There are many levels and grades of transmission. There is a very light transmission that can happen just by being in the vicinity of a realized person. It might happen in our dream. There are also very strong and powerful transmissions. These we call Shaktipata and this is a strong foundation of and in non-dual Kashmir Saivism.

The guru usually looks for people where the Force is already unusually strong (like Morpheus sought to find and awaken Neo) and strengthens it when certain conditions allow. The whole process is bound up a bit by protocol. Of course the guru would like to ignite everybody but it simply doesn't work that way. Even if he or she could, it can't be done like that. We are talking about a very strong current of energy for which the body, and especially the nervous system, needs to be slowly prepared. The student has to start with a drop. And then another couple of drops, before sipping.

The flame needs to be nurtured. There are strong winds. Something needs to be built up and protected. It really needs to be built up first. Many people give it away again too quickly. It requires a relationship of love, loyalty and respect. Most important in Tantra philosophy is that the recipient learns not to ask for him or herself. There must be a very strong inclination to be of service. To help other people. The Seva has to be strong. This is very important for the ego and we see what all this means in this movie. Although everybody who watches the movie, of course, identifies with the heroes – the Jedi – a tantrik is very much like them. There is a code of honour. The Jedi is not aiming at accomplishing personal goals.

A Jedi has a strong intuition, although some things are very hard to sense. He does not only operate in the world of the known and things that can be seen and heard by ordinary people. He trusts to be guided by the Force and lives in the here and now. Intelligence is however fully functioning. The love, devotion and loyalty must be pure. This person must be a vira to overcome all fears and doubts. Death must also be inquired into.

In traditional Tantra training, several practices are performed in the vicinity of corpses and graveyards. There is a stronger opening between the seen and the unseen world. There is, so to say, a lot of spirit-traffic. The tantrik specializes in bridging both worlds as they affect each other. It is very much a matter of tuning in and being fearless. Only people where the Force is already very strong qualify for a more intense training in Tantra.

We are talking about a lifelong training program. A very special mission. There are no negotiations. It is a life of service. No compromises. This book is merely a preparation. We are just trying to find some suitable people. It doesn't even have to be that many. There are many tests and I have had severe tests myself. Tests I would very much hesitate to give others. It requires operating amidst total chaos. When you cannot handle it, you would go down into deep and dense confusion. It is possible that you will not come out.

A tantrik is really a combination of a genius, a saint and someone who is a bit *off*. I explained before that a genius, a psychopath and a saint are very closely related. The movie 'A Beautiful Mind' portrays how this man is first a genius at maths, then becomes schizophrenic and later on in life becomes saint-like when things settle down and he learns to master the mind. The arousal of kundalini affects every area of your life. You will become dispassionate with the world. Your intellectual capabilities might strongly increase. It really is a philosophy of love and peace. First the mind and the ego have to be well trained. It really requires someone who is a master all the time. A master over the inner forces.

We all have different talents and capabilities. We are all a flower that is capable of fully blossoming. We are a mirror that can be cleaned. A diamond that needs to be polished. A block of confusing marble that hides a great sculpture inside. The Force is in everyone. It is merely a matter of recognition. Surrendering. As I have stated so many times, we need to tune in, develop our finer antennae and become very strong and steady. To become part of the Resistance (Jedi), we need to be very resistant. We need to become immune to chatter and gossip. 'Negative forces' should not get a grip on us. We need the right discrimination and to choose a life of joy and service. That service may require us to suffer. That takes a hero. A hero is not someone who is a hero when the circumstances of life are pretty. You have to be steady when things turn out differently as well. To not lose faith. Amidst difficult circumstances. Sometimes, it requires tough decisions. We certainly have to investigate our personal desires and aims in life. Who is it that 'rules' us?

A hero is someone who is willing to step out of the way. So that the Force can fully make Itself known. That requires total clarity. We have to do very thorough self-inquiry to arrive at that state of powerful inner clarity. We need the heroism to ask for guidance and help. There is only very little that a human being can do by him or herself. But it is said that when we take one step towards God, She takes a hundred steps towards us! How hard it is however, to take one step.

I sincerely hope that we will manifest a powerful team of very pure Jedis. All are welcome. Let's start with diving and drinking. Soak it all in. Demand more from yourself. Don't be lazy. Be willing to do the work. This path requires a superhuman effort. Any mediocre effort will fail. The powers of maya are very strong. A life of surrender is much more difficult than a life of control. At least in the beginning...

Rebirth

Kashmir Saivism is not only a matter of 'unplugging', as you can see in the movie The Matrix. There is a very thorough training program involved with many tests and initiations (loading programs).

In spirituality there is a problem or challenge. The challenge is that we start to approach spirituality, realisation or liberation from the mind. The mind – due to its very nature – can never understand and certainly not experience what the true meaning of spiritual life is. It can only form ideas about it. The mind needs to be silenced in order to walk through the gateway of mysticism.

We have used the word 'the mind' so often. What do we understand the mind to be? The mind is not the same as the brain. The brain is a physical organ located in our head. The mind is not localised although its function seems to be centred in our head. When we talk about the mind we do not usually point to our toe, elbow, back or heart. The mind is a certain energy. The mind is in itself difficult to understand. Why? Because we basically only know how to function with and through the mind.

We have to be able to step out of the mind in order to understand what it really is and this is the problem. People cannot. They are stuck in their mind and glued to the matrix. The mind is the creator of duality. It is all our thinking. It holds ideas and concepts. It has expectations and desires. It holds all memories. It creates a sense of separateness. Even our entire perception runs through the mind. Without the mind you would literally see an entirely different world. The world is as I see it.

The mind judges. It feels lack. The mind makes associations. The mind makes us believe that we are not good enough. That we need something like enlightenment. The mind is quite a trickster and we need to learn how to settle it down. We have to learn to silence the mind.

The mind identifies and we have to learn to de-identifv. We identify with the mind and the body. We feel *mine* and *thine.*

In a non-dual teaching we have to learn to bypass the mind. To come to direct cognition. But how to go about this when people come to learn spirituality with the mind? They read this book with the mind. It is the very mind that approaches spiritual life. It is the mind that engages in meditation practice. In Kashmir Saivism we explain that all these efforts are rather futile without an infusion of Shakti.

Shakti is the Goddess.

With the infusion of Shakti, the spiritual process starts to unfold. With Shaktipata our life will become a meditation whether we want it or not. With Shaktipata – even when we are not going to meditate – we will fall into meditation. Kashmir Saivism is centred around Shaktipata and Shakti is the river. It is the divine stir. Shakti is the world-process (maya). Shakti is Shiva. Shakti is kundalini. The guru is the carrier of Shakti. He/She is the bestower of Divine Grace. It is the guru-principle that will set us free.

You think or hope that it is your own efforts, but all your efforts will make you spin. A human being by himself can only accomplish very little, and this is a hard nut to crack. This is difficult to swallow. This is something that you do not want to hear or understand. That you are not that powerful. It is Morpheus who sets Neo free. But it would be nice if you co-operated. You need to be whole-heartedly dedicated to this affair. It is a love affair.

On the Path of Yoga, Beauty & Delight we do not seek *fame or fortune.* We are not even after 'success' or 'happiness'. Success and happiness are mediocre states. They all pass and wither away. One day we are successful and the next day we are a failure. Everything in this world is transitory. Except for our soul. Our soul is the ever-lasting link to the Divine. It is a small flame with the potential to turn into a blazing fire. Success is sometimes a curse. You might be better off with a life of failure. So why complain? Consider the fact that your entire life is a blessing in disguise.

Tantra is a cult of the Goddess. This is the Way of the Ancients. In the past the people all over the planet worshipped the Goddess. With the word 'worship' I do not mean a primitive, dual worship but a full blossoming of respect. It is about living in harmony and accepting the mysteries of life. It is an inner alignment. The Goddess is the bestower of wisdom. Wisdom is the only true liberator. Pure knowledge is the only thing that will set us free. Happiness and success are just another fix for the sleepy and drowsy ones. Happiness and success are food for the ignorant. What is the golden calf?

What the world really needs is a restoration of the Goddess. People have almost forgotten Her. And the result is that the earth is withering away. On the news you hear about the increase in floods and fires. The face of the earth is covered with war and exploitation. Those are not the ways of the Goddess. The ways of the ancients are a full blossoming of our inner faculties. Men have great respect for women, as they are the carriers of the Goddess energy. This ultimately leads to divine infusion by tantric rituals of lovemaking.

But my friends are you willing to give up something? Entry into this Kingdom is not possible as long as you cling to your mind and its ferocious ideas. You'll have to leave your entire indoctrination of superiority, spirituality, Christianity, Hinduism or Islam behind. You must enter naked. When you are ashamed of being naked you need to do more self-inquiry. Where does the guilt come from?

So, as long as you are in this only with your mind we cannot make progress. The guru-principle is looking for those few ripe souls who are dedicated, steady, loyal and who want to learn surrender and practise devotion. We need open hearts. Only then can this guru-principle enliven your buddhi. Buddhi is the only chance you've got. Buddhi is your higher mind. It is also pure logic. It is like the soul (over mind). When buddhi enlivens, kundalini starts to stir. Tantra-philosophy is about fire. A small flame that can grow into a fire. A fire that becomes the sun. Shakti re-uniting with Shiva. It is not the trendy new age paradigm of going from our head into our heart. No! Kundalini-sadhana is about piercing all the chakras. It is the snake that comes alive and devours us. It is offering your head to the Goddess. It requires heroism.

If the teaching is understood by a mind only, it'll be a disaster, just as Christianity has become. JC was a great master but many of the disciples had a Taliban-mentality. So the transmission is a great challenge. How to pass it on? This we call the guru-sisya parampara. It is very precise. In Kashmir Saivism it does not go as you think or imagine. The master will shake the disciple. Shock. Until the mind settles down. Only when there is some steadiness can the real teaching begin. The real teaching is not for the mind. When the ego is still strong it is simply dangerous to hand over the secrets.

So you have to do the preparatory work. It is the guru-principle that will do the surgery on you. This surgery is necessary. But you have to give inner permission to cut away that which is not real. That is what the guru does. It can be a totally painless operation unless you choose to resist. The guru works from the inside. But you have to practise devotion, make sure you become steady and practise sadhana. Yet, your intellect has to understand these writings. In the Path of Yoga, Beauty & Delight experience and knowledge need to go hand in hand to later culminate and explode in wisdom.

Religion

Someone asked me whether The Path of Yoga Beauty & Delight is a religion.

It all depends a bit on how we define that word. Several experts talk about Tantra as a philosophy and I took on the same habit. I call it a path but it is also a movement.

The word 'religion' is usually associated with a dual philosophy. A non-dual philosophy is rarely called a religion. Buddhism is also not considered to be a religion as they deny the existence of God and a soul. Vijnanavada Buddhism is a non-theistic philosophy. Advaita and non-dual Kashmir Saivism are theistic. A theistic philosophy can be personal or impersonal. In Kashmir Saivism God is transcendent and immanent. This means that God is not outside of creation, as if He was only living on a cloud or at a certain address in Heaven. God **is** the creation. But God is not only the creation. He or She is the beyond. That which is before time and before anything at all. Even beyond any category like space or void. God is the experiencing consciousness and the silent vibration.

Non-dualistic Kashmir Saivism explains all of this in great detail with Paramashiva, Shiva-tattva, Shakti-tattva, the five elements and also with the principle of Spanda, Mesa and Unmesa, the operation of maya and the five powers of Shiva.

Kashmir Saivism is non-dualistic, but for the most part Saivism is dualistic. The schools of Saivism that are dualistic are religious. The same cannot be said of non-dualistic Kashmir Saivism. Many people however have religious associations with the word 'Kashmir Saivism' and that is one of the reasons I choose to continue with 'The Path of Yoga, Beauty & Delight'.

According to Tantra-philosophy, the world is not an illusion. It is not something that we need to deny or renounce. This is not a nihilistic philosophy. The body is regarded as a temple. Sexuality is not something to renounce as evil, bad or a sin. Tantra is a philosophy of sublimation. Things that others consider to be bad are used in Tantra-philosophy to overcome all distinctions of good and bad, as they are part of dualism. Tantra is the yogacara: the path of union and integration. It is the only philosophy that does not create a split personality because of the above-mentioned reasons.

Kashmir Saivism describes evolution from the Big Bang to the next dissolution and beyond. It explains how a stone is an expression of consciousness and so is a fish. It has a very thorough understanding of time and space. It describes which sadhana is most appropriate in which phases, and also distinguishes different practices for men and women of different calibre, always emphasising the operation of Grace.

Some people also remarked upon my distinguishing between people – some being very good and others unworthy. Try to understand that what I am bringing is authentic Tantra philosophy. Tantra is not merely about making love. The rituals that involve lovemaking are only for the vira. They are commenced at a certain stage. They have to be practised in the energy-field of the guru. When a pasu engages in these rituals, it might very well lead to his downfall. We must differentiate between a pasu, a vira and a divya.

A pasu is the animal-like man. He is guided by his lusts, 'lower' emotions and ambitions. There is a lot of inertia. The guru can see this in his energy-field. According to general Tantra-philosophy this person has to start with the lower practice, like meditation and worship. The panchamakara (ritual with the five forbidden substances) is only for the vira. When this ritual is commenced externally, it is considered to be left-handed (vamacara).

To come across a divya in these times of Kali Yuga is very rare. A pasu has mainly tamasic tendencies. In a vira, rajas guna is strong. A divya is already very pure and sattva guna dominates. As I said previously, the intermediate goal of sadhana is to strengthen sattva guna. In a divya the sense of egoity, separation and dualism is virtually vanished.

In a pasu the impurity (mala) is still strong. The best way to transform this is through diksha (initiation). Diksha is with mantra. Mantra is part of mysticism in Tantra. Mantra carries the energy of the Goddess. With mantra the sadhak performs certain worship. This often involves yantras. Yantras are geometrical symbols. The guru chooses a certain deity for the sadhak. The sadhak builds a relationship with this deity in his sadhana. In proper worship, the sadhak unites with the divine. This is the stage of the divya whereby the worshipper becomes the worshipped and all that remains is worshipping.

This man or woman lives her entire life in meditation. Every word is a prayer and every action is worship. The sadhak is granted the boons of the deity. This is the tantric way of accessing hidden powers in man. Tantra is about the full blossoming of our hidden potential. It is about realising the divinity within. One of the most powerful mantras in Kashmir Saivism is 'So-Ham' derived from the Hamsa mantra. So-Ham means 'I am Shiva' (Sivoham).

Kashmir Saivism makes us realise the divinity and the unity of the 'separate' tattvas. It is not an intellectual process, but based on actual experiencing. Shiva descended down into stone, and it is our task and opportunity to ascend up and to integrate all the tattvas back to Shiva-tattva and beyond (Paramashiva). This is not accomplished by thinking about it. It is not a matter of dry and abstract philosophy. It has nothing to do with dogma. It has nothing to do with positive thinking, programming or conditioning. Reading books won't make it happen for you.

For some people the entire process happens through Grace (intuitively). Most are guided by a guru. The ascension process is done consciously. It happens over a multitude of births. If you have a strong recognition, it is very likely that you were involved in this sadhana previously. The guru-principle will find you again in your next incarnation and start with where you left off in the last life. That is characteristic of Kashmir Saivism. The purpose of sadhana in Kashmir Saivism might be described as to free the sadhak from all impurities, tendencies, karma, vasanas, impressions, illusion, ignorance and suffering so that only the real remains. During this process the sadhak will gain certain powers and his or her potential will come to full blossoming. Because of the dissolving of ego, these powers can come to benefit other living beings and the evolution of all, not only mankind. The result will be balance and order in the entire universe.

The Jedi-knight is the protector of this balance and order.

The human being has to step out of all conditionings and that is what a tantrik does. This path is about a life in service. It is not about victory for the morals of the ego. The tantrik prefers to offer all of his or her own tendencies to the fire so that the Force can operate fully through him or her.

May the Force be with you

The Guru-principle

The guru-principle is certainly visiting some of my readers. In most it doesn't feel very comfortable. Too low self-esteem. Not enough determination. Too proud. Too full of your own ideas. Too much holding on. It wants to talk to you and share something with you, but most of you are too busy. The guru-principle is none other than Shakti. She wants to live in you, awaken you and lift you up, but many lack devotion and gratitude. So this energy finds someone else to live in. Don't think that it will come by every month to see whether you are ready. It is an unprecedented opportunity.
For Divine Madness to grow in you, you must be willing to lose your mind. Any feelings of superiority or arrogance will not do. You need to offer all tendencies of the small individual

self into the fire. You think you need to take care of *this* and *that* but why don't you set out to discover how God takes care of you? That does not at all mean that you become passive and inert. Allow your life to be invigorated. There is (latent) fire in the wood, but when it is not ignited, we cannot fry an egg on the log. Attune your life to the Goddess. Determination also means watching yourself to see where you drift off into a blue pill. With a blue pill there is no Self-remembering.

Devote your life to the Goddess. She is all that you are anyway but when the devotion and steadiness rise, she also rises to come full circle. She is in you but not making love in you yet. The cosmic love affair still has to start. Right now you have your own *love* affairs. Your affairs with money, power, jealousy, control, hate, right and wrong. You are attached to some small things. There is no desire to be crushed underneath the feet of Shiva.

It is the Shiva Nataraj who crushes the ignorance in his eternal dance of life. The feet of the guru are the highest concentration of Shakti-energy. That is the best place to dwell. No matter how often he or she washes his feet, there will always be dust underneath the feet.

Tantra philosophy is a noble way of living. Current civilisation is very uncivilised. Agent Smith talks about this with Morpheus up in the skyscraper. For the animal-man we have religion. He can get his teeth into the dogma and fundamentalism that it offers. The vira has to become free of all the conditioning. He has to learn to use his common sense. Pure logic needs to arise together with recognition of beauty and a blossoming of the arts. Tantra is about the unfolding of our inner potential. Not with NLP-techniques, but through mysticism. It is wisdom by direct cognition and inner knowing. This requires the slaying of all mind-tendencies.

We are members of the Resistance. It is a dangerous life. If your own individual desires and ambitions are too strong, you are not going to make it. You will long for a big steak, just like Cypher. You must remain steady even amidst false accusations. People will leave you. You will face troubles and obstacles. You must get used to the Ways of the Ancients. Many of you think that life will turn out to be a big party, but are you prepared to suffer if that comes to you? Many people in the West like the new age ideas of *shaping your life, as you want it.* Creating *your desired reality.*

This is nothing other than the rape of authentic spiritual philosophy and wisdom. It will propel you much deeper in ignorance and suffering. And the founders of these ideas, who are good marketers, continue even though they know that even their top-trainers and authors are not living the life of their dreams. In order to live the life that you dream you only need to dream. And dreaming is what most people do. When you dream you are processing unresolved stuff.

But how will you dream when all is processed and resolved? You don't need to work too hard but can relax a lot more. If only you would be totally relaxed, all would be fine.

But it is hard to relax. It is difficult to settle the mind down. There is a pain in our back and a lot of tension even in our pelvic region. But most of you when you relax go into a doze or start dreaming again. I am talking about a state of being alert. Multi-dimensional awareness. Tantra is very much about developing your will power. Very much! AND about being relaxed and alert. This is all about mastery. Mastery is the cosmic love affair. It is Shakti uniting with Shiva. This can only happen consciously and full circle in the nervous system of a human being. And it happens by Grace. But your intellectual understanding and your sadhana will facilitate the process to take place in the most beautiful and optimal way.

There are several inferior states of 'enlightenment'. The Kashmiri Saivist does not settle for them. She is not lured by psychic powers. The Kashmiri Saivist is well trained to avoid the traps. The Matrix is an entirely inner movie and Neo does very well. Most people take the exit too early. There are many things to learn for the spiritual aspirant. It is a process over several lifetimes and most people are far too impatient. Hypocrisy is not allowed. Hypocrisy is not part of authenticity so we should be on guard for trendy statements. Hypocrisy is a cancer that can grow and kill.

We should not be afraid to use the sword. Let the sword fall where it wants to fall. It is a present from the Lady of the Lake. This is no kindergarten. Mirdad also went to visit a monastery at a high altitude on the top of a steep mountain. There was no path leading there. To get there one has to travel barefoot at night without a torch. Authenticity means we make no compromise. When you are part of the Resistance, there are certain rules. There is an unspoken order. There is a certain protocol.

This is not a new age hotch-potch. Nobody is forced to enter the Resistance. One must want it for himself. Only the hero joins. You have often been warned. There are many spiritual organisations with beautiful and elaborate teachings. No need to say *yours is bad and mine is much better*. This Tantra-philosophy is certainly not for everyone. If you prefer fundamentalism, there are so many things to turn to. Tantra is very un-dogmatic. For a certain celebration you may be asked to dress in only yellow, or to make yourself very beautiful. Maybe you are requested to wear very little.
You must be willing to be grinded down. You may also fight. Lovemaking is not only tender or aloof. This is the dangerous life. Tantra is walking the razor's edge. According to Marx, religion is opium for the masses. Tantra is about waking up from your sleep. It is about Self-remembering. Pratyabhijna is the quintessence of non-dual Kashmir Saivism. But many people

suffer from low-self esteem. We are looking for people to become a master. But what does that word mean? 'A master'? A master of one's own fate? A master of my destiny? Master over others? Master of *myself*? Mastery over the inner forces? Master as the other side of the polarity?

Mastery is the full blossoming of all of our bodies. It is the opening up of the rose. The rise of Ma Kundalini. The piercing of the chakras and the knot. It is unleashing the star that you are! It is about reaching for the stars and beyond. It is spreading. Expanding. Weaving. Mastery is the operation of Grace. It is redemption. The result of the resistance is freedom from slavery and oppression.

Tantra is also a discipline. It is a system for the physical, psychological and spiritual dimensions. Tantra is the philosophy that teaches us how to enjoy the beauty in the maya. Tantra is a philosophy of acceptance. Nothing is to be rejected or renounced. Everything is to be appreciated and valued because of its divine potential. Tantra is about healing. Tantra is Living Water. Tantra is mysticism whereby that which is spiritual can live together and be combined with that which is material. Tantra is also self-inquiry. It is practical in its application and sublime in its aspiration. It brings a message of hope to a humanity that is suffocating in its own problems. Tantra is about consciousness. It is a preparation for the awakening of universal consciousness within.

So when you are not yet aware of your mastery and divinity, you make yourself into an aspirant. The guru does not see you as a beginner or a *silly* aspirant. He sees the flame of divinity within you. That is what he makes rapport with. The sword of the guru cuts away that which prevents the flame from shining brighter. Let's call this ignorance. So the guru-principle *liberates* itself just as ignorance destroys itself ultimately and 'you' are merely watching. This is all Grace in full operation. Can you feel it? Watch and enjoy the process! Don't *think* you are, but **know** you are!

The Guru-principle Internal and External

Kashmir Saivism is a non-dual philosophy. The guru and the disciple are a sort of polarity. As I wrote before, the disciple is the beginning and the guru is the end.

Many people have strong hesitations with gurus and for very good reasons. Although Tantra describes many characteristics of a guru, it is very difficult to spot a good one. We could say follow your heart, but unfortunately your heart is often 'wrong', although all experiences are useful. You need to take your time to get to know this person better but that is often not easy or possible. Some say that you need to examine their disciples, but usually all of them have some very good disciples. When the guru is married, you could check out how they are together and it might give you a clue. Ultimately, the proof of the pudding is in the liberation of his or her disciples.

Many enlightened or liberated people teach a system that is directed and aimed at the higher chakras. However, the problem in general for people who are looking for spiritual advancement lies in their 'lower' chakras. How to deal with power? How to deal with sexuality? How to deal with masculinity and femininity? How to deal with challenges in relationships? How to do self-inquiry? How to break through mental barriers (conditionings)? How to become freer? How to come to full realisation?

The most important thing is how we can combine our life with spirituality. In fact it is a matter of infusion. And in fact my next advice is very important, although many will put it aside. Spirituality is a very slippery path. There are really many very liberated souls and enlightened teachers. When you are a good painter it does not imply however that you are also good at teaching others how to paint. This is very important to realise. Not every good salesperson is automatically a good manager.

You are not looking for someone who likes to be adored. You are not looking for someone who likes to tell all his or her own ideas or experiences. You need someone who can guide you to liberation from where you are now! When you want to travel to Timbuktu, it will not suffice to meet someone who knows Timbuktu very well and tells you about the beautiful lakes and mountaintops surrounding Timbuktu. That is what many spiritually inclined teachers do.

This guru-business is very delicate. A certain population feels drawn towards having a guru. You must have noticed that some people feel proud to say that S or Z is their guru. I really want to warn you. The person in whom the guru-principle operates strongly needs to be very steady. When one operates as being a guru, there are heavy responsibilities involved and you must really know what you are doing. Many people operate as a guru when it would be better if they had stayed at home, or gone fishing.

It certainly is not a competition as to who gathers the most disciples. It is not about binding people. It should have nothing to do with a dependency relationship. This is all-important to understand, since we are in a somewhat Eastern tradition and, as I said before, all Eastern traditions are based on the guru-disciple relationship. This is true for Sufism, Advaita Vedanta, Tantra, Zen, Buddhism, Vaisnavism, Saivism etc. Having a guide is important somehow.

It is virtually impossible to find a qualified guru in Tantra. There are thousands of men and women who would want to be your guru. Virtually none of them knows what Tantra is about. The knowledge that people in general have about Tantra is extremely fragmented. Most tantric gurus are either centred in their higher chakras or they are very much centred in their lower chakras. Those centred in their lower chakras can come across as very powerful and charismatic. But they may not be the vira. Others are very much in their higher chakras. They have a beautiful teaching but not the teaching that most people need.

There are many reasons why things can go very wrong. In many groups people lose themselves and they learn very much to rely on the energy of the guru and the group. But you have to become strong inside. You first have to discover yourself and become yourself. In many groups it becomes a mess. Very often the guru tells everyone to live a celibate life. This usually leads to a lot of suppression and denial. Celibacy is a wonderful thing when it comes automatically and is natural, but for most people this is not the case yet. The other extreme is that there are no impediments at all and that many relationships break down.

I am not saying that a relationship is the highest aim in life. How do we relate to God however? In one way an important relationship is with your guru. It is beautiful when you feel you are married with him or her, but not when it destroys your other relationships! Be very careful of this. The relationship with your guru has to strengthen and intensify your love for everyone. Challenges may always be there. Make sure you have at least the former (intensification of love for everyone).

The relationship with the guru is a mystical one. It starts in the external realm and will grow into an inner one dissolving in 'the end', which is merely the beginning. There is not much to say about it. Morpheus and Neo are a beautiful example. There are many beautiful examples of people who are not in their bodies anymore. It is interesting in a way to build a relationship with someone like that. It is sort of secure and romantic, but it is more important to be with someone who is alive. 'Dead gurus don't kick ass!'

When you have found one, make sure he or she is a bit funky. There has to be recognition. Different cults and sects have different 'rules' for a guru to abide by. In left-handed Tantra this all becomes a bit complicated.

A tantric guru has to be powerful and wise. Powerful not so much in the ego-sense of the word but energetically. Most guru-types will however also be strong personalities. This is inevitable in order to shock their students into awakening. They should not ask money of the disciples, although in the west it is a bit more complicated these days to have a roof and food. It is nice to have a guru who is original and authentic. If I were you, I would choose someone with a good sense of humour and who is not too serious all the time.

A guru is usually from a lineage unless he is an avatar. An avatar is generally someone who is born free. Swami Nityananda was such a one. A guru is either initiated by his or her guru or everything comes by Grace. The latter frequently happens in Kashmir Saivism. I know of one 35-year-old guru in Kashmir Saivism who is very bright and a top body-builder.

Some people have been excellent teachers in the line of Gurdjieff without having met him. Swami Nityananda passed everything on to Swami Muktananda. Muktananda was a very scholarly person. Well versed in the scriptures and sadhana. Because of the initiation of Muktananda on the deathbed of his guru, he received mythical powers. These powers, which are none other than Shakti, beamed out to his disciples who had profound experiences of Shakti. Some people teach similar things as Muktananda without ever having met him physically.

Wherever Muktananda was, people felt touched. Mystic occurrences happened. People started to shake or had powerful experiences of kundalini. These are signs of a guru carrying strong Shakti-energy. And that is in fact all that the guru is. The guru is someone who is very alive and awake. Don't create too many stories about it when the truth is simple. It is said that Muktananda passed Shaktipata to thousands of people. That was a light version of Shaktipata. An authentic guru can only pass the real and strong Shaktipata to a couple of disciples – as far as I am aware.

Very often the initiation or Shaktipata starts to work later on in life and not immediately. Swami Brahmananda Saraswati Jagadguru Bhagwan Shankaracharya of Jyotir Math initiated Maharishi Mahesh Yogi in Sri Vidya. This is the meta-science that provides intuitive knowledge of everything in the world of form and of the entire beyond. Long after his death, Maharishi kept on having more and more profound and deeper cognitions in the nature of Reality. This happened when his people practised strong sadhana and he went into silence. Then he often came out with deep revelations of the Veda. I explain this to you so that you understand that this is not the way we know in the west, which is book knowledge attained by objective study.

My general advice for Westerners is to be very careful with gurus from the US and from India. It is my experience that Americans are too much marketers, and for Indians it is difficult to bridge the gap between the East and the West. The Indians are very attractive, but their teachings are usually not suitable at all for any Westerner to follow. Too easily they assume that something that would work very well in India will also be very effective in the West.

Very few are ready to renounce the world or to live a celibate life. Devotional practices like singing mantras and bhajans often don't work very well here. Selfless service does not work well in the West. The mind is exceptionally strong, as is the hesitation and doubt. Westerners in this era are not interested that much in ritualistic things, although they find them charming. They reject anything superstitious, although they are very interested in mysticism.

The year 2002 in Amsterdam is an entirely different experience than Rishikesh in 1600. There is a lot of evolution in the world of form these days and this has to be taken into account in order to bring people from the world of form into the Nothingness and back. Tantra is not about denying the world of form, and who would want to? The Path of Yoga, Beauty & Delight is for the modern man and woman who want to live 200 % of life, but who are most of all determined to push through to the highest levels of liberation that are possible. It is an integration with and in the world.

On Kundalini

Evolution is a process of cultivation of consciousness in which we discover another possibility in the series of transformations, namely from man (automaton) to superman (the Perfect One). Tantra leads us to the full blossoming of all potential by awakening the kundalini-Shakti. Unconsciously this may be happening anyway, but a sadhak does this with full awareness and does it speedily. Through sadhana, the tantric practitioner realises universal consciousness.

Tantra arose out of the playful nature of Creative Intelligence realising through a clear, clean and alert nervous system that the root of the universe is Ultimate Reality, which is one without a second, and therefore my/our own real and true nature. This Reality for Tantra is called either Shiva or Shakti, both of which are identical as the moon and its beam. This Shiva and Shakti are the static and kinetic aspects of the one Reality.

As in the moving wheel, there is a point, which is static, around which the whole wheel moves. In the same way, Shiva is the 'static' aspect of Reality around which the dynamic or kinetic Shakti moves. So Shiva being a static aspect of Reality is considered the centre of the Universe as a wheel.

This Shiva is playful, and although he is totally fulfilled within himself, he wants to experience Himself even more fully even though He already is totally full. Thus he wills (Iccha tattva) to be many. His willing then issues forth in a projection (Jnana tattva) in the form of Shakti. Through an intricate process of seeming creation, he projects the entire universe as an abhasa (projection, maya). Shakti manifests herself in the planes of consciousness or lokas. These planes of consciousness are not one and the same; they differ in the degrees of density of matter out of which they are composed. The creation is, however, not different from the Creator. The creation manifests in increasing degrees of density or complexity. This is called the descent into matter. All matter is, however, maya and Shakti. This process starts from the subtlest element and culminates in the creation of gross worlds, that is prithivi (the 36th tattva) which is composed of the densest matter.

This process of creation takes place in the macrocosm and the microcosm simultaneously. The Yoga in the Path of Yoga, Beauty & Delight is based upon the principle of microcosm and macrocosm, meaning that all that is contained in the universe is also contained in man. This is to be experienced outside of the mind by experiencing. This is what we call 'Walking the Path'. A man or woman who is thus totally awake and functions with full multi-dimensional awareness is 'holding up the glass'. An ordinary human being is considered to be asleep because all of his or her powers lie dormant at the base of the spine. Besides he experiences only inferior states of consciousness and does by far not access his fine potential. He lives in the magic universe of the mind, which is ultimately not real. Kundalini yoga deals with the expansion of inner latent powers and awakening.

The same universal consciousness expresses in minerals and men. They only differ in expression in the levels of consciousness. Tantra leads to what Gurdjieff called man #5. Tantra is the key to the highest civilisation. That is to say, our body is also made up of the same five gross elements. There are many rivers in our body. The brooks meet at certain point or junctions, which we call 'chakras'. These chakras are centres of consciousness. They can be compared to powerhouses by which each and every cell gets its power. But how does this power flow?

There are 72,000 nadis flowing through the body: an intricate network of energy, invisible to the external eye, and also (as yet) to modern technology. The nadis are very subtle veins, like a hundredth of a hair's breadth. Through them life currents (the Force) flow and vitalise the body. Without the Force or Shakti, man remains an automaton.

The Sahasrara is where the manifestation of consciousness is at the highest level. Tantra considers this to be the abode of Shiva. The lower spine (pelvic region) is considered to be the abode of Shakti. The latent Kundalini can be awakened through determined sadhana and/or by Shaktipata. When the awakened kundalini reaches Shiva's abode at Sahasrara, the sadhak has lost all self-identifications and ignorance and experiences full delight (Satchidananda). This is similar to the ascension where a link is established between the earth and the heaven. Earth is symbolised by the 1th chakra and Sahasrara is the heavenly abode.

While ascending, the Kundalini absorbs all elemental forces, which are ascribed to the centres. At the Sahasrara she absorbs herself in Shiva. This is experienced as cosmic intercourse and is the true Tantra. Here nectar is issued from Shiva known as soma or divine ambrosia. Kundalini (Shakti) absorbs this nectar and comes back to her own place, which is the Muladhara-chakra. In her descent, she revitalises all the centres with the ambrosia. This process of Shakti going upward and coming down after union with Shiva has to be experienced again and again till a stage comes when she rests permanently with Shiva in Sahasrara (Mt. Kailash) and the descending movement stops once and for all. This depends on the intensity and competency of the sadhak.

Such a sadhak does not utilize the awakening of Kundalini for his or her own pleasures, but for the liberation of all humanity. In the same way Lord Buddha did not want to keep the gem of liberation and Self-realisation for himself, but wanted to share it with mankind. In Tantra we do this in a tantric (viracara) way.

Applied Kundalini

The term 'Yoga' in the Path of Yoga, Beauty & Delight not merely denotes *union* but it also represents the process, which leads to union. As I wrote before, there are many practices of yoga (Raja, Hatha, Bhakti, Karma, Jnana and so forth). On *our* path we practise all, but most are a preparation to ultimately go to the sadhana of kundalini yoga.

The kundalini yoga of Tantra philosophy is the same as looking a lion or a snake in the eye. Not everybody is advised to wake up a sleeping bear! But some people, like Tristan in the movie *Legends of the Fall,* have that calling. This process is extremely difficult (and *dangerous*) but it gives everlasting eternal joy to the sadhak. The pre-requisite for the process of awakening the kundalini, is guidance by an expert who should be well versed in this type of practice, and who can efficiently guide you until it comes to natural fruition. One needs to already have a high level of purity in the mind/body complex. Another pre-requisite is strong will power or firm determination.

At the base chakra *the door* must be opened. That can be done in a ritualistic way, by Grace and/or by ardent practice. Arthur Avalon describes that the sadhaka sits in a prescribed asana (bodily posture) and steadies the mind by concentrating between the eyebrows. The sadhak engages in a certain kind of breathing by which intense heat is generated inside the body. This draws kundalini upwards. By mental concentration with the aid of mantra, the jivatma – which has the shape of a flame – is brought down from the heart to the Muladhara. There it is re-united and moves along with awakened Shakti.

The key point here is that in the ascending journey she absorbs all the gross elements ascribed to the centres (chakras) and then bathes in ambrosia issued by Shiva in Sahasrara. In the return-journey she revitalises all the centres. This entire process endows the sadhak with the following qualities: When it attains to Sahasrara on its upward journey, the sadhak becomes completely liberated from the limitations of mind-body and space around. On the return-journey while passing through the Ajna chakra, it endows the sadhak with the quality of success of words, meaning that whatever he/she speaks turns out to be ultimately true. It confers the Vak-siddhi.

When it passes to Visuddha chakra (throat area), it endows the sadhak with a unique type of oration in which (s)he keeps the hearer spell-bound. When it passes through the Anahata chakra (heart), it confers the unique power of discrimination by which the sadhak comes to know what is true and what is false or what is eternal and what is non-eternal. When it comes to Manipura chakra the sadhak is endowed with the knowledge of the various vidyas or abilities which will express themselves spontaneously. When it passes through the Swadhisthana chakra, the sadhak is endowed with poetic sense and the subtle techniques of yoga. When it comes back to the Muladhara chakra (base of spine) the sadhak enjoys good health.

There are further siddhis to be gained by the sadhak, which are all to be understood as signposts along the way towards total liberation, initiation into the mystic realm and joining higher ranks of the Resistance. These are powers, which normally do not manifest in a layman. They manifest only after piercing one after the other centre. At the end of this process, the sadhak gets totally transformed. He feels the presence of the supernatural energy of Shakti within him- or herself. He or she – as in Tantra there are many advanced female practitioners – is taken into the mythic teaching and School of the Goddess. Some are entrusted with the sword of Excalibur.

But my dear friends when the mind is *the boss*, all this will not happen. We first have to become less busy with the world of maya (matrix). That is the first step towards freedom; you have to see things for what they are and not for what they appear to be. Things appear to be all sorts of things in your mind but it is only outside of the mind that you can recognise their true value. Merely reading these words and thinking about them is not enough. *The problem* is not in the words but in the mind that interprets them.

The mind is a strange thing; it abuses you, makes things that are not there and it holds the key to liberation. It is your worst enemy and can be your greatest ally. An advanced mind can give you beautiful 'spiritual experiences'. However, many of these spiritual experiences aren't worth a dime, while kundalini is your very life.

Speaking & Whispering

We are all servants. Mostly I. Really. I speak the truth when I say that I would like to be a servant. Merely that. I bow to the divinity in you. You are divine. And I bow to That. But I only bow to the master. The master does not need to bow to the servant. So when I bow to you, I bow to the master in you. That is what I am holding on to. That is what I wish to connect to and make rapport with.

Oh yes, I also like to dance. As all energy, I like to move. When I move it is in a rhythm and in a dance. It is a celebration. A delightful experience. In this dance I like to destroy. Destruction is beautiful. Not only would I like to destroy cancer, the illusion of death, fear of the unknown, arrogance, low self-esteem, superiority, ignorance, rivalry, hate and separation; I like to destroy the tension in you also. It is this tension that is holding the illusion in place. It is possible for you to realise how deluded you were. And, upon waking up, to realise the eternity that you are. Time itself is a sheath. I would like to take away the veils in front of your face. I sense that there is a beautiful face behind those veils. I feel two deep eyes and lips I would like to kiss. I feel a heroic heart that wants to beat forever. But my dance is in another rhythm.

I would like to dance with you. To take you away out of *this* world and into mine. My world is so beautiful. There is such a relaxed sense of enjoying. There is a great view from here; the entire world rolls out beyond. I would like you to float with me. Floating in endless space on a divine rhythm. When all tension would release from your body... If you dare to hold on to Nothing only and allow yourself to fall into my arms ... I would fall with you and teach you how to enjoy falling. The joy of letting go. There are so many things I would like you to let go off.

I also wish to make you pregnant. I want a baby to grow in you. A new birth. An inner explosion. But first I desire something else to die. I would like to murder the false self in you (ignorance) and then see a divine birth. A new body of light. That body is sooo beautiful that I already wish to dance with her right now. I desire to drown in her deep eyes of golden colour. Her flame pulls me closer. Her hips rotate mine into a spin. I am lost by her beauty. I have no more control and she comes even closer. She demands something of me and I try to feel what it is. Are you with me? She is whispering something in my ear as well as she does in yours. What is She saying to you?

Please close your eyes and tune in!

Fear of Committing

Some people have difficulty in committing themselves to someone they love. This is portrayed as being a psychological disorder. That is certainly possible but we should also understand that it might be something very wise. Other people and also psychologists sometimes tell us a lot of crap that we believe. In our self-inquiry we have to be very fierce. That means not only examining why we are afraid to bind ourselves, but also we need to investigate MUCH deeper. Why should we bind ourselves to a person? What or who should we be committed to? FEAR means False Evidence that Appears Real. Investigate the false evidence. Why should you bind your love to one person exclusive of others? What is the fear involved here? We really have to go much deeper!

We are all involved in a journey towards experiencing much deeper and more profound love. It is an expansion of the heart. We need to push through the false evidence. If you are not willing to investigate certain things, your full love might not be released, although ultimately it will be. Isn't that what you really want deep down inside?

Contemplating means you do self-inquiry in the sense that you try to work something out, but then you also let it rest and sink in. You allow some 'freezing' and 'unfreezing'. You let it linger. You make room for the Grace of God. It is self-inquiry together with prayer. With prayer here I mean silence.

Most of us think we have to work it all out on our own or with the help of another person; that we have to do it all by ourselves. But make room for the soul. We are using such a tiny fraction of the powers that lie dormant in us. We cannot awaken them by force. It has nothing to do with hype. Many new age people have been trained in the paradigm that they can create whatever they want. God does not come into the picture here. But my friends, you are surrounded by great powers and in you are also great powers. We hardly know the influence of the stars and planets on our lives. We live in a web of radiation. We are a bundle of frequencies and we are affected by frequencies. This is all a huge play of energy.

The thoughts of an average person are rather unimpressive. Yet a human being has great possibilities. We do not only have an instinct but we have 'thinking'. We can create. We can do self-inquiry. We can get depressed. There are thousands of examples of human beings who became liberated or realized. We are not amidst this glorious creation to become depressed. Human beings can produce great pieces of art. We can expand our consciousness infinitely. We can access great powers that are hidden within and put them to work for humanity. But we have to start where we are.

If now we are mainly concerned with our own wallet... If our major goal is to increase the size of our house... When all we think about is making love to Richard Gere or Pamela Anderson... Most people who go on vacation find the quality of the food to be most important. Surely the soccer scores are very interesting. Most people want to be happy. I don't think that that was the mission of Jesus Christ. His main thought was not what to eat next or where to sleep. He was very concerned with humanity. Some of you look with one eye at the person with whom you are talking and with the other eye you gauge the movements on the stock exchange.

All I am saying is that if you are very concerned with yourself only, you ought to do some more contemplating.

Soul – God

So my friends, let's talk about a daring subject in divine philosophy: what is the relationship between men and God? What is the relationship between the divine flame in men – the soul – and God? How does the small flame relate to the big flame (fire/sun)?

There are basically three views (derived from different experiences). One school says that they are separated. This is basically dualism. Their explanation is done in different ways. Others uphold the principle of the co-existence of sameness and difference. They say that the soul of man is qualitatively the same as God but not quantitatively.

I don't care whether you are a dualist, an atheist, an Advaitin, a gnostic or a Vaisnava. We are all human beings involved in a journey where our fate is connected. Our destiny is intertwined. We are either going to make it together or not at all. It looks however like humanity is not going to make it. We are in drastic need of leadership. People seem to be waiting for something (remember the Oracle to Neo: "You've got the gift but it seems...").

All of my writings and efforts are to invoke that leadership in you. And of course there are many people on other parts of the planet who are coming to the same answers. Because they have raised the same questions and did the same inquiry. I am not talking about politicians. I am talking about brave human beings. Heroes. Those who dare to stand up and those who have the intelligence to bow down. Experts in consciousness, is what we are looking for. This is a training school in diving. Maybe Osama Bin Laden had his men trained to become pilots and to commit suicide. I am however not talking about revenge. I am talking about the power of love.

Really excellent divers are able to collect pearls. Those pearls we do not hang around our necks, rather we infuse the power into society. But first we have to become good divers and learn to breathe well. We must even breathe well amidst difficult circumstances of life. Breath is life. This Life force should be able to grow and dispense evenly. Amidst pain and pleasure. Most people are upset by pain and pleasure. They desire more pleasure for themselves and want to reduce their own suffering in any way feasible. They would even be willing to drink the blood of another. I am saying that you have to be willing to give your blood to another. When you are afraid of a small prick in your upper arm...

Use all your faculties. Visualize the Force, feel it and draw it in. Let the Force be there when you eat and drink. While making love. Allow the Force to move in you. Let Her move you. Allow the Force to re-invigorate you at night. Walk with dignity. Don't act like you are an ignorant human being. Feel how you are blessed already and be grateful. This is one of the most important things in spiritual practice. Many people are not making it because of impatience. They do not realize at all how they have grown tremendously and they want to go faster. Be grateful and be willing to go slowly. Take people with you. Stabilize. Be steady. Throw some offerings into the fire so that it can burn even stronger. Caress the flame. Feel the connection of the flame with the mighty fire. Are you willing to dance in that fire?

I also wanted to write a little about the words 'being drunk' that we use. I am sure you understand it has nothing to do with alcohol. It is a flow-state that we enter by surrendering. The real beauty of life can only be experienced upon surrender. But this is very difficult for people. It scares us; we don't want to do it. We want to be in charge and in control. If we are not, God knows what will happen... And indeed it is so! We can feel powerful from the ego, but that power is very transitory. A man may be very wealthy but in five years he can be broke. The economy is very unpredictable. You can be the CEO of a huge corporation but if the numbers are not good for a couple of quarters they will dispose of you. And where is your power then?

We need to strive for authenticity. Authenticity lies in surrender. The mind only knows fake love, fake honesty and fake self-knowledge. Unfortunately, it seems that we as human beings need all kinds of experiences before we come to consider surrender. It is a hard process of unlearning. Of letting go. But once we discover the joy of surrendering, life becomes so beautiful. A mighty force starts to flow and we accept. We do not strive for fame and fortune. This joy of surrender is what we call being drunk. It is a state of ecstasy. It is the state where the sun devours the flame of the candle. A dance affair with the Beloved. Sometimes She unveils Herself in all Her magnitude and splendour and we are simply swept away. Then for many days She is gone and all that remains is the bittersweet memory. We cannot force Her to come out. We cannot find Her. She is on the hunt for you.

This is the game of love and you have to learn what it means to become a lover. It has nothing to do with the rules of society. Successful people are usually bad lovers. It is the people whose heart has been crushed many times but who keep on living and loving. Their hearts become free once they learn to forgive, to understand, to let go and to grow in love. Take all the experiences of life. Forget about labelling them as 'wrong' or 'bad'.

It is a magical universe. What seems to be your worst nightmare might turn out to be your greatest blessing. In Tantra nothing is rejected as bad or wrong. Nothing is of no use. How could it be when all is Shiva? The entire world process is none other than the great Goddess. If you reject a part, you reject the whole and She cannot reach you. Welcome everything.

Welcome adversaries. When someone knocks on the door, you open it with a warm heart. Be alert. Don't distinguish between this guest and the other. If you welcome wealth but reject poverty, you are just showing your ignorance.

I know this is hard, my friends. All of society teaches us certain things. All the media write about the same thing. Nowhere do we read about wisdom. But in your heart you know. Don't let society corrupt you. Be as pure as you are. You are a child of the Divine Mother. Let her caress you. Surrender into Her arms. Take care of your brothers and sisters. Make sure everybody has something to eat. So many people have wounds. What everybody really wants and needs is your love. It is easy but the mind makes it hard. Be united. You are the conqueror. Conquer hearts. Investigate all feelings of jealousy. Try to rise above them. Don't get swept away with childish thoughts. Reclaim your dignity. Don't be happy with a stone when you can swim amidst the jewel of the Nile. Love is there to share and to multiply. Don't try to hold it in a rotting pool of stagnant water.

Let it flow freely. Conquer the mind. The mind wants to claim. It wants to possess. It creates 'me' and 'thou'. 'us' and 'them'. Make life into a dance. Feel the great and mysterious love affair.

Self-inquiry

Thinking and wandering is not the same as self-inquiry. Most people say that they are willing to go all the way in self-inquiry. Going all the way in self-inquiry is in fact the same as taking a red pill. It is the same as 'unplugging'. It is coming to full realisation. But all the way is all the way. It means the slaughter of the 'automaton'. It is the victory of the Conqueror over 'the animal'. It is the defeat of the small individual self. It automatically gives rise to surrender. This path is only for the vira. It is what we call viracara. Vira means 'hero' and cara means 'path' or 'way'.

But the human animal protests heavily when he is brought to the slaughterhouse. It yells and screams. It does not want to let go. He wants to hold on to the illusion even though he says he yearns for truth. And what is the illusion he insists on holding on to? It is the illusion of keeping his life in place. He clings to the muds of ignorance, like jealousy. Jealousy is part of the animal. There is no rational explanation or justification for jealousy. There is no wisdom in jealousy. It even has no beauty. It has no grandeur.

In Tantra the disciple willingly offers his head to be chopped off by the Goddess. This exemplifies his yearning for freedom and the truth. This shows his heroism. The conquering of wisdom. A vira is someone who watches the automaton continuously. The automaton is fishing to take over all the time. One moment of forgetfulness and the automaton is in charge again. That is why Gurdjieff stresses the importance of continuous Self-remembering in order to give rise to man # 5.

'The animal' is a bundle of thoughts, ideas, reflexes and conditionings. It is the shadow and thus the cause of hate, revenge, shame, guilt, perversion, hypocrisy and corruption. We need to bring in the light of awareness. But the animal is very clever. And when we think it is gone, the animal is in fact only hiding. He strikes at a moment when we are tired. When we have had enough. When life is seemingly not fair. When we feel betrayed. When we perceive injustice. But the vira is the conqueror of the animal.

The vira has steadiness. The vira exemplifies 'Soul over mind and mind over body'. The vira does not lose himself in animalistic tendencies like gossiping. The vira is uncompromising. He is not affected by the normal viruses, that sleeping people carry and pass on. The vira is a servant of love and the conqueror of the animal. He knows that human words are a movement of air. His knowing is not in the mind but of the heart. No words can shake his loyalty and commitment. He is a warrior that fights with a code that is not known.

The vira protects love and not false possessions or ignorance. Ignorance is what is sacrificed. The vira offers the ego to be chopped off, the animal to be sacrificed, and he sits on top of the automaton. The sadhak practises observing. He engages in self-inquiry. He practises self-control. Yet he might engage in bhoga as well as yoga. Both are part of his discipline and life-style. The sadhak has an attitude of acceptance and gratitude. He upholds wisdom and liberation. Many automatons are programmed for 'honesty' but they live a life of deceit.

Most people approach spirituality through their glasses of morality. The book knowledge supersedes experience. The enlightened ones are based in experiencing, but they disagree on how to bring people who are glued with the mind to the matrix of duality to the other side. There are many approaches possible.

As people have different tastes for food, as they prefer different kinds of music, as they like different styles of painting; in the same way they have a different way of talking and writing about what they consider to be the ultimate truth. It is for this reason that Morpheus says he cannot explain it to Neo but that he has to experience for himself. But only when he is willing to find out how deep the rabbit hole goes.

The rabbit hole is about falling and tumbling down. Yet human beings hold on. They like to be in charge. They want to have control. But who is in control of the automaton? That is a question that people haven't figured out yet. The automaton is a script very much like the matrix. Bringing in awareness is freeing the actor from his prison (role-identification). It is stepping into the unknown. We cling to the known and are afraid of uncertainty, while liberation lies in the embrace of the unknown.

Yet how difficult is the unknown. As soon as life presents us with an opportunity to experience the sacred unknown, we immediately try to kill it by making a decision that creates another prison of seeming certainty, or we continue to live in our projections. And thus we chain ourselves in the dirt of the known. Proudly we continue our life wearing the emperor's clothes. In our clownesque performance of 'spirituality' we even take on a master. But as soon as we see another master driving by in a bigger car, we try to jump in his trunk hoping he will take us there.

According to Maslov we have to first satisfy the 'lower' needs, like a roof, food, comfort and belonging. Then we proceed to build the ego with things like 'status' and 'control'. This takes us on a tremendous trip. If we are lucky we learn to conquer ourselves and tread the path of self-actualisation. This is the maturing of the evolution of man. We can however not tread this path steadfastly when we are still very busy with our ego-needs. We must be very certain what it is that we want. Most people project childish ideas onto the master or guru. Or they linger in their ideas of infantile grandiosity. Tantra is for the girl who has grown into a woman. It is for the boy who has become a man. But these days people are thrown back in between the one and the other.

You must know who you are, but many people sometimes feel like a grown-up, at other times a child, later on a nobody and sometimes they feel mastery rising. But they cannot hold it. It comes and it goes. We have moments of brilliance and of blind stupidity. Sometimes we are very sure and at other times we forget. Spirituality is not merely an act of giving meaning to our life.

Spirituality is about knowing who you are. Self-knowledge comes upon self-inquiry. But the key to self-inquiry is transcendence, to go beyond. We start to inquire anywhere in the mind or the matrix but ultimately our inquiry has to lead us out. The purpose of Tantra is to shower you with divinity. Divinity is the profound experiencing of ecstasy, insight and wisdom. Ecstasy is freedom. Knowledge is bondage. That is why we have to be very aware of which path to tread and in whom to have faith.

How does Tantra work?

Tantra is not merely a philosophy. It is not merely a science. It is indeed about esotericism, mystery and magic. It is about love and wisdom. Why do I emphasise Tantra? Tantra has a long-standing history of worshipping the Goddess. Human beings strive after happiness, but all happiness that they can find is transitory. There is no lasting happiness to be found in the external world. There are many pleasures and each of these pleasures carries the seed of pain. Everlasting happiness is not to be found in duality, as in duality everything comes as opposites. With happiness comes suffering as well. The more we discover we know, the more we realise that we don't know. So how to access wisdom? Pure wisdom. Untainted wisdom!

This has been the quest of tantriks and rishis for ages. They have designed a very intricate system for the full unfolding of the human potential. It is based on mysticism and encompasses initiations and energy-transfers. This is all stored in lineages. Tantra uses the sacred power of mantras and yantras. Nobody who is merely curious will ever understand how all this works. That is the brilliance of these masters. It is a very well kept secret.

Not every reader has affinity with this mysticism from the masters of the Far East. And you don't have to. There are plenty of ways. You don't have to follow anybody. All is stored in you already. Sometimes Grace comes to us directly. The supreme path is the pathless path. But who is ready for that? That is for the divya in whom sattva guna (purity) strongly dominates. That is extremely rare. In the divya 'the curtain' is easily opened and the Self blazes forth. They need no practice. The highest 'path' in non-dual Kashmir Saivism is based on complete surrender. It is the fast track.

The guru is the one who carries the Shakti-energy. This person becomes like that through intense sadhana, by initiation or by a direct intervention of Grace, a combination of any of those. The guru is sometimes translated as 'a teacher'. But this is not a teacher like we are used to. It is not a teacher who teaches through the mind some stuff that he or she gained in a study with book knowledge. The guru teaches outside of the mind. For some people this is very confusing because it is not what they are used to or what their mind feels comfortable with. But mostly the guru is translated as the remover of ignorance. Remember that the first sutra in the Siva Sutra's is 'Knowledge is bondage'. What do they mean by this statement? That all knowledge in and of the mind further binds us down. Only the Truth sets us free. Only pure knowledge is liberating.

This pure knowledge is not book knowledge but Shakti-energy of the Goddess. The Shakti-energy and the Goddess are one just like heat and fire are the same. Book knowledge generally contributes to avidya (ignorance). This might be a bold statement but consider it from the viewpoint that it (knowledge in and of the mind) is fragmented. No knowledge is total or complete. Except Vidya. Tantra is about this knowledge of the sun. Even a student of Tantra cannot access this Vidya. A student approaches life, Tantra and the guru from the mind and he or she seeks to make progress with the mind. The mind however is the 'cause' of apparent bondage.

The disciple is the hero and the lion, who feels a strong calling in the heart. Usually these kinds of people have done many things; they went to several groups, did therapy and coaching. Past-life regressions, NLP, Avatar, Reiki, meditation, sweat- lodge, talked with angels and studied many things. After some time they experienced how difficult the task at hand is. They come to understand the power of Grace and surrender. Usually life forces them that way. They lose feelings of superiority and arrogance. They become humbled. They start to lose their ambition and religion. Life takes a strange turn. Especially when their heart is crushed a couple of times, they allow the life force to take over and it swells up in them. Compassion and universal love rise naturally.

These people are less busy with personal gain and accept a simple life. They live more reclusively, or focus on helping other people. Both are fine. Some semi-enlightened people believe that helping other people is in vain and is just an act of stirring the illusion. Others feel that reclusiveness is egoistic. It all depends on the inner state and attitude. Helping others can indeed be an addiction. Living totally aloof, simple and alone can be a very high state of awareness and enlightenment.

Maybe there are 14 dimensions in life. Maybe you only know level 7 and 8. Maybe dogs hear at level 6. We do not perceive sounds on that level, but through technical instruments we know that they exist. A cat may see things on level 9. The fact that we do not see it does not mean that there is nothing there. Our sensorium for perception is just very limited. It would be very ignorant and stupid to maintain that there is nothing else (than 7 and 8) based on our mind-perception. A lot of my work has to do with helping people to access other states of consciousness. We try to train our senses to see, feel, smell, taste and hear more. With more fullness and depth.

It is not that interesting to believe fairy tales from someone who claims to have access to level 11. Because until you experience it, they are fairy tales. It will be interesting for you to expand your consciousness. It is highly interesting for you to become more aware. It is a breakthrough to experience 3-D listening. Expand it further. This expansion comes with deeper relaxation. Deeper relaxation with heightened awareness. That is all that I am trying to help you with. You need to try and practise sadhana and you must open yourself for some help from 'the other side'. This is part of mysticism.

It is not very useful to try to cling to old-fashioned and hypocritical rationalism. I am not that impressed with science, dogma and religion. The white people developed great science indeed. But how would the world be today if the white people had not been so expansive and dominating? If they had been a bit less greedy and not tried to force their own shit down the throat of every living person on the planet? All organised and institutionalised religion is from the past 2500 years. How was it before that? Was there only barbarianism? Hedonism? Paganism?

We are so proud of our current civilisation. There are so many technical breakthroughs and lots of comfort for many people. Especially a few 'privileged' ones. Are you ready and willing to see what is really happening on this planet? How is the willingness to share with each other? Sharing was very natural for 'primitive' civilisations. How is the sharing in the West? The system really has you and you are not even aware. The matrix is very real. But also here we see that people are hardly willing to let go of anything. Buddha gave up ALL his possessions. JC lived a most simple life sleeping under the tree. A swami basically means a monk with no possessions.

This path of YB&D (Yoga, Beauty & Delight) is for the householder. But when the practitioner is very busy with expanding his estate, little room is left to expand consciousness. There are certain laws. When you sit on the toilet the sewer is below and the life is above. But many people make the life above into a sewer as well, and they are not willing/interested to discover the divine life that exists inside. They prefer the big promises that the matrix gives in the external realm even though the results are devastating. We still believe in the illusion of money, sex, power and fame.

Problems ... #!*^...

A philosophy should be practical. We have to be able to use it and to apply it to defy the problems and challenges that we have.

I know very enlightened and realised people who have challenges. It really depends a lot on our attitude/viewpoint/state of consciousness. With regard to *solving problems*, we could talk about:

- cleaning up the mess in our lives
- becoming steady, clear and responsible
- developing our will-power and creativity (being pro-active)
- learning from adversaries and advancing accordingly
- working through the karma in our lives
- living in harmony with the laws of nature
- accepting whatever comes our way
- sublimation
- *swallowing the world*
- 'unplugging' and being absorbed in the Self

You see that it is not a clear-cut answer. It depends on where we are. Some people need to learn 'responsibility'. They have to develop their will power much more. They need more determination. This is one 'end' of the scale and I am not saying that 'the scale' is real. All is part of *abhasa*. The other side of the scale – for people who have practised **lots** of sadhana and self-inquiry – is detaching from the maya and its *problems* and being very much in Self-referral. There is not even 'an act' of detaching, since our mind expanded into the sky of infinite consciousness.

For most people I would strongly suggest working with the first four points. I 'must' also point out the existence of the other points, which will become a reality for us once we do the proper homework and exercise spiritual self-effort. Remember that when we take one step towards God, He will take a hundred steps towards us!

Let's briefly highlight some possible problems that people experience. They could be of a financial nature. Many people are experiencing relationship-turbulence. People feel stuck/depressed etc. Many issues are connected with low self-esteem. There are health challenges. We might not be able to get a job. The job maybe isn't going as we want. Family-problems exist. We may not be able to express our emotions or talents. In addition it is possible that we *suffer* from impatience, vengeful feelings, injustice, jealousy, anger etc. Let's look at a couple of these, and forgive me if you find these topics to be too *earthly*.

Problems of a financial nature

Mostly the solution here is to live a more simple life. Scale down!

Relationship problems

There are always *challenges* in this area. In our love affairs there is attraction and repulsion. We all need to grow in emotional maturity. This comes with age and through reflection. Many problems are caused because we have many expectations, projections and unresolved or repressed memories. Crises help us to reflect. Our projections are glued to the feelings with unresolved negative energy in our unconscious mind. We can use any and all projections for self-inquiry. In this regard people say that our relationships are a mirror.

There are books to write about 'relationships'. We usually forget to reflect on our most important relationship. When we focus on and build this most important relationship, all our other relationships will flower.

Stuck / depressed

It is good to realise that animals are not depressed. It is a typical human trait and comes about because we think and have a mind. This mind goes on wild trips and we become depressed. We have to learn to be steadier. We can also realise that there are external influences like the tides, the moon, atmospheric influences and many others that affect our state. We need to grow larger than our beliefs, superstitions and conditionings. And in saying this I am not denying that certain influences exist. Tantra deals with all of them.

Low self-esteem

Make sure you understand that everybody is basically suffering from low self-esteem because we identify with the mind/body. We forgot our real nature and suffer amnesia. In this amnesia many people also have a psychological low self-esteem. All this results from poor self-knowledge. People keep hanging around in their fears, projections, ideas, self-pity, irresponsibility, guilt, doubts and what have you. They say they want to make progress, but the truth is mostly that they don't. They really like these feelings. They feel so familiar. They would hate to experience the unknown. Because that is crazy, of course they say they are looking for help and a cure. But all they want is a sort of *fix*. They do not want to go to the root. Even psychologists do not want to. Nobody wants to, as that would mean suicide. So most people prefer to fool around a bit even if this 'bit' is five years of psychotherapy. People are extremely attached to their minds and the matrix (maya). They refuse to let go!

Health problems

Some health problems we cannot cure or improve upon. Most we can. We certainly can learn to accept and to be more creative. We can do much better self-inquiry as to the cause. For surely everybody can live a much healthier life! We all know what it means. But bluntly we lack will power. We are like Cypher and prefer to have a steak. So please don't complain when you don't have a pro-active, responsible and super-healthy life-style.

Problems with our job

Work hard and as perfectly and with as much awareness as is possible. Focus on maximum added value to your employer and customers. Do not go with power-games, gossiping, being lazy, complaining or wasting time. As a result you will either make promotion or you will be kicked out. When you get kicked out and have this attitude, I am sure you can easily find another job. When you are looking for a job you should either create one or shape up your attitude and be more creative.

Family problems

Family problems can be of a different nature. With sincere health problems and old age you should give all the help that you can and that is welcome. Culture (worthwhile customs) is also very important. The general advice is not to try to change your family, but to love and accept (encourage) them. For family problems of an emotional nature, I refer you to the section above and remind you of the importance of becoming totally clear with your father and mother.

Not able to express our emotions and talents

It is VERY important very important to be able to FULLY learn to express your emotions and it is also VERY important to come to a total expression of your talents. If you don't use it, you'll lose it. There are hundreds of thousands of trainers and coaches who can help you with this.

Impatience, vengeful feelings, injustice, jealousy, anger etc.

They all have to be processed. It requires self-inquiry and all of the other things that I wrote about until and including the practice of Kundalini-yoga, deep purification one way or another.

These were some short notes on 'problems'. Very often we need the intelligence of a good chess-player. If that is not possible, we resort to *bhakti* (devotion).

French, Swedish and Chinese

I asked people what the greatest wish of a good teacher of French would be. Most people answered that it would be that the whole world would learn to speak French. But that is unrealistic. The people will never all speak the same language. Some will speak Spanish, some will speak Russian, and some will speak English etc.

The great dream of an excellent teacher of French is that one of his students will also become a great teacher of French. That would be such a blessing. And that is really my hope. That some of you will become great masters in the Order of the Holy Fire. This is what we all desire. This is what the world needs. We are the blue connection. It is a love-injection. Try to not only read these words, but to soak in the energy. It is mainly a process of absorption.

But we need to sacrifice all the time. Most people are still too arrogant. All these tendencies of supremacy have to be sacrificed in the inner fire of Ma Kundalini. You need to put new wood on the fire. The wood is all the projections and jealousies that you still have. The masters of the far East have a strong and world-encompassing vision, but the core group of people has to be very strong. I want you to become great dancers and most people still need thorough training to become free. There is the possibility to be great lovers of life and many of the readers still need to work through many conditionings.

Our *guru* is the music and our sadhana is to dance. It is our destiny to be an eternal dancer. But do you hear the rhythm of your heartbeat? Many are so locked in to the outside world. There is so much talk and way too little silence.

All the time there is structure around you. In the West there is hardly any escaping. You *have* to do the groceries. You meditate on the floor, sleep on a mattress, and sit on the toilet. There are sounds and images. Feelings. We use language. The moon and the stars are the jewellery of Lord Shiva. The words appear by His Grace. Some people battle with words. Others find Grace hidden in them. It is all a great mystery.

The essence of sound is silence. The essence of movement is stillness. What is the essence of words? Can you find the breath inside the breath? Don't blame the structure, as all is a manifestation of the great Goddess. The way to Shiva is through Shakti. Have you contemplated thoroughly what this means on different levels?

'French', 'Swedish' and 'Chinese'... they have something in common. There is music in language. Great poets in every country have been able to put the Inexpressible into words. They wrote divine poetry. Divine poetry is outside of the mind. Can you read in that way when you are reading anyway? Can you make love while you eat when you are eating anyway? Can you make your work into worship when you are acting anyway? Can you really float while making love?

Some people just want to add. They already know a lot and want to see whether they can learn some more by reading this book. But, dear readers, that is really not the purpose at all over here. The door is everywhere but you are not seeing it. The door is a magic one. You can pass through it, but you will have to leave your mind behind. No book can teach you this. Are you striving after happiness? What is so important about your own happiness? Which lasting happiness do you hope to find? Where? How does happiness relate to wisdom? Do you feel that you are blessed when things are going *your way*? Why did Neo not choose the highway? Because he had been there before. He knew where it was leading. He chose wisely 'our' way. The difference is a '**Y**'. Look at that symbol What does it represent for you? 3, 2 or 1?

My dear friends, beloved brothers and sisters! It is time to make another step. I invite you to make a heroic step. Many of you know so much. Make a gracious step towards the Beloved and drop the knife. Stretch out your hand and be willing to tumble. I like to see trembling legs. Security and the known feel nice and safe to the ego, but I invite you to let go of your images of God and to tremble in His vicinity.

Somebody told me that she was willing to do sadhana and self-inquiry, but wanted to make sure in advance that the end would be very nice. She didn't like how the crew of the Nebuchadnezzar had to live. But there are no promises. Morpheus did not promise Neo he would end in heaven. This path is only for the very few and I have emphasised again and again that it is dangerous but people don't take that seriously. They think: 'Yeah, yeah, I can handle it!' Most people suffer from overestimation plus low self-esteem.

You have to investigate the darkness and I am not saying that there will be light, peace, love and harmony afterwards. When there is a knock on the door you should open the door and welcome the guest whoever it is. She might speak Swedish...

Interface

Since many of you are so fond of labelling, I have invented a new label for you. Many students on the path have a strong preference for talking over silence. They need to be requested to become silent, but we never have to spur them to talk. That comes automatically and here we have precisely the 'problem'. The automaton!

These automatons have a lot of theories. They know a lot about things.

The problem in the Matrix – as you may remember – is that 'the machines' became very smart and powerful. The world is in great danger now because of the entire automation-process. Many automatons are without awareness. They blindly follow some programming. Because they follow blindly, it is a shadow. The Resistance is about the rise of the Conqueror. The restoration of Shangri-La (Zion). You have to become a strong flame yourself. That is your task.

Every automaton needs an interface. Otherwise it just keeps rambling and rattling on. An interface connects one or several pieces of hardware with software. All are good systems by and of themselves, but without the interface there is no proper communication. I wrote before how religion is actually 'to link'. The music is the guru and the listener the disciple. The listener needs to learn how to merge into and become the music.

I am just a guy who helps people to learn to listen to music (an interface). In Tantra we are not in favour of fragmented knowledge and this is the main reason that it is and has to be an oral tradition from master to disciple.

People are not interested because they can get everything on the internet. Well ... search! Search for all the things on the internet. And what will you gain in the end? RSI? An expanded head? Don't tell me that this is your path towards wisdom? When you really understand where the wisdom resides, you will immediately see the superfluousness of the internet. No 'thing' adds to wisdom. All 'things' have to be inquired in to. All 'things' need to be seen for what they really are. Many things need to be unwound. Who is going to teach you that?

If only I could help you to learn to really listen to music ... We could be listening together for days, weeks and months. Listening and dancing. Gurdjieff also devoted the last period of his life to teaching people how to dance with the Gurdjieff Movements. He was a great Master of Dance. Also I can probably still grow in my receptiveness to surrender to music. Never think that you have 'got it'. I can probably give any reader an experience to hear music in a much more refined way. 'The more I hear, the more I hear there is to hear!'

This is really Yoga, Beauty & Delight whereby the listener evaporates. It is magic. Several musicians and DJ's produce music that is really outstanding. Never before in human history have we had the opportunity to hear music in such a divine way (because of the way we can record, master and play it). Oh, before people could hear music much better than we do now. They had much better ears. They could hear sounds in the jungle. People were much more attuned to life. People these days are fairly blunt, numb and dull. You need to understand much more about words, talking and language and for that you have to practise *mouna* (silence).

We are just going to do something very simple: to listen to music in its most naked way. Bare and stripped. Totally present. Virtually nobody has received the gift that the musicians have made for people. People are busy talking and they even talk while relaxing and thinking that they are listening to music. Most just hear some echoes in their own mind. Many people first have to learn what an in-body experience is. In Kashmir Saivism 'contact' is very important. You must have contact with all the elements and really train your senses to the utmost. Much refinement is needed. Do not regard the body and senses as you, but as instrument for experiencing.

My entire teaching is really a lot about refinement. There are great opportunities to learn at hand. To learn something very rare. It is about weaving a Magic Carpet. But it requires much of you.

Our Way, your Way, the Highway, the Fourth Way

Good luck with thinking your way up to wisdom.
There is another way, which is 'our way'.
Our way is the fourth way.
What is the first, second and third?
How about 'waking', dreaming and sleeping?
What do we call waking? Waking is an operation with our mind and senses in a certain 'world', which we mistake for real.

I would rather you focussed more on dreaming. Dreaming is a wonderful state. Why don't you enjoy dreaming more? Don't reject a dream as 'false' too quickly. From which standpoint is it false? What exactly is false and what is real? People presume that the waking state is real. They pride their rational way of thinking. I would rather you practised a bit more philosophy. Plato already told of this with the shadows.

When you start to investigate the dream, you will discover an in-between state. This in-between state is the doorway. It is very subtle. The body has to be very relaxed in order to find it. It is hidden. Morpheus: "The matrix is a world that has been pulled over your eyes to blind you from the Truth". Neo: "What truth?" "That you are a slave Neo. You were born into bondage".

It is too bad that I am mostly with people who so much enjoy waking, dreaming and sleeping. Especially waking, they think is very wonderful. Kashmir Saivism is a very direct way. All that is needed is recognition. It is the doctrine of recognition. Technically we call it 'Pratyabhijna'. You need to be made ready to see. Many of ~~you are~~ afraid of pain. You live with many fears. Yet everybody desires to be fearless. Nobody likes to live with fears. We live in a world of right and wrong. Good and bad. And what do we fear? We fear losing our identity. We fear losing our religion.

Waking up or unplugging is losing the religion. Letting go of all false beliefs and superstition. Realisation is razor-sharp. It is not a fluffy new age state of a(nother) dream amidst a dream.

The world is sound. Everything is sound. There are so many frequencies. What frequency are you? Do you vibe on hate, war, conflict and jealousy? THE MUSIC IS THE GURU. MUSIC IS THE ANSWER! You need to attune to the music and then the music will do its work on you. Music will liberate the world. But you need to learn how to listen. Real listening is a no-mind experience. When you are a no-mind, the music will tune you. Meditation is the experience of the primordial sound. You need to become that sound. Fascination for music may help you.

Many people, however, are too much in bhoga. They are not willing to do the preparatory work. Many people are merely enjoying life, or trying to. This is not the way to eradicate the ego. Others live very ascetic, monastic and celibate lives. Many people live in a confused state in-between. The point is not just to go nuts on music. You have to use music as a meditation and thereby it is indeed possible that you experience profound ecstasy. That is Yoga, Beauty & Delight. Yoga is however the first of these words.

The fourth way is beyond. It is turya. It is the observer of all observers.

The Magic Lens

Shiva descends from the pure void of undifferentiated consciousness through very fine levels of consciousness into gross form. This is a very mystic process that cannot be described in gross language. The job at hand is for the human being to ascend into these finer and most refined states of consciousness (Wonderland). That is the process of completion, which is actually one of absorption.

This process of descent is not one of transformations. When Shiva 'becomes' the 36th tattva, his original substance (no substance) is not lost. It is Shakti that seemingly changes form. Shakti is the world-process. That is why all people on the planet speak about Mother Earth. So Shiva remains Shiva throughout the entire process. Shakti is Shiva. There is nothing that is not Shiva. In this field of pure potential (Shiva) there is a stir. This stir we call Spanda. It is a movement that is not a movement. This movement that is not a movement is interesting. Tantra is about this movement. This movement can be experienced when we fully explore our (states of) consciousness. When there is stress in the nervous system however, we need to work through it so that we get access to Wonderland again.

The human being is a sort of mini-Shiva. It is very condensed consciousness. Consciousness that lost its non-dual awareness. It lost all access to wonder and magic and now it is stuck in the 'real world' of the senses, mind and elements. As if a prism lens of the mind is put in-between and now everything is experienced as duality. The task for us is to bring our mind to more refined levels of consciousness (or to allow this to happen). Therefore we need to make our mind steady. We have to become one-pointed and discover how deep the rabbit hole goes. This is necessary to enter the lens of the prism. Our mind has to become as steady and pure as the one beam that goes into the prism that splits the beam.

Wonderland is not for the doubter, fearful one, 'realist', scholar, sheep or the big ego.

One beam enters the lens and an entire world is created. Who and what is the human being in this total picture? This cannot easily be explained. We can slowly prepare ourselves to come to full understanding. This understanding comes about by experiencing. In order to come to experiencing we have to investigate the personality. We need to strip it layer by layer so that we come face to face with the lens. We can then decide whether to step through it or not. This process needs to be guided by proper understanding all the while, and that is what the non-dual philosophy is for.

Experiencing comes about by stepping through this magical lens and then looking back. What you will see is amazing and indescribable. I would like to take you there. By 'there' I mean in front of and vis-à-vis with this magical lens. It is as Morpheus told Neo: "I can show you the door but you are the one who has to step through it!"

So what does all this mean for us? That we need refinement. Refinement in our behaviour and thinking. Tantra is very much about refinement. Refinement in our perception. Refinement in the way we listen to music. But we also have to release the beast and the animal. We dance in ecstasy, write beautiful poetry and produce great works of art. Practise philosophy. Become the Lord of the Rings. Feel your body. Tune in very well. Feel changes in atmosphere. Sense the higher energy, soak it up. It is not a matter of the mind but of absorption. This is the same as reading vs. drinking the mails.

This all requires a balance and an interchange between male and female energy. We need steadiness and determination. We need an incredible will power. AND we need absorption. Delicacy. Tuning in. For women I have described the process of being a Goddess. Men do not need to emphasise the 'beast-aspect' too much. That is too easy for the man. Man needs to grow in sensitivity. Both are aspects of the same energy. The Goddess will function through men and women, but in a slightly different way. She brings the potential to fruition. When the subtlest polarities are blended, the Ardanarishvara arises. Here Shiva is half male and half female.

There is a lot of goldsmith work (blending) to be done. But we need to prepare ourselves. We start with the blacksmith. The blacksmith is about welding. Of course he also hammers. Only an Arthur can draw Excalibur. Why? Because he is pure of heart. He pledges loyalty to protect the mystic school of the Goddess. He is committed to differentiate real from false and to bridge the old ways and the new ways.

We live in a world of form and know somewhere that the essence of form is the formless. We live amidst matter, and quantum physics makes it very clear to us that the essence of matter is non-matter. We know from astronomy that we are merely a tiny piece of dust in the big picture. So we live amidst a great trick, which very few people have 'solved'. Morpheus tries to make it clear to Neo, but even with someone as highly evolved and extremely bright as Neo, it is difficult. For the mind Wonderland is and will always be difficult.

The greatest Indian philosopher is considered to be Adi Shankar. In Kashmir Saivism we of course adore the great Abhinavagupta. Abhinavagupta was trained by several masters in a broad range of philosophies ranging from dual to non-dual. Adi Shankar wrote a dazzling philosophical work called Vivekachudamani. Only very few people dared to translate it because it is so complex and refined.

It seems that Adi Shankar wrote this complex work at the age of 11. How is this possible? No westerner will understand this. Their imagination is destroyed at a young age. This is the work of mysticism. I could give you a detailed explanation of how it goes. It is the result of the guru-disciple lineage. It is the river that flows out of the hair of Lord Shiva.

It is known to many that Jesus was trained by the masters in the Himalayas. He probably had a guru there. In this tradition we often refer to the guru as our father. So who is 'my father in heaven'? The guru – I tried to explain many times – is a principle. The guru is the liberator.

So, to return to the topic of this text, you have to learn to sense the energy that the guru or your master is carrying. A master in Kashmir Saivism is someone who is loaded with Shakti-energy. He or she carries a mighty flame. It is this fire that can ignite your fire. We are looking for people with energy. Not spiritual zombies.

In the East it all goes rather differently. A person is thirsty and tries to get his thirst quenched by different groups, schools, philosophers and teachers. When all that does not work, he goes to find a master. This can take many years. The master usually sends this person through difficult and sometimes lengthy tests. And then finally he is given the nectar to drink. And only then the nectar is felt and experienced, as the heart is now open and longs for the sweet and soft rain. May this Grace fall upon your heart.

Touch

We operate in the world with our senses and mind. The mind categorises, interprets, gives meaning, stores memories, fantasizes, holds concepts and ideas, identifies, justifies, links, doubts, fears, rejects, desires etc. The mind is an extension of the matrix. Most of all, the mind splits Reality into two.

Morpheus invited Neo to stay in Wonderland, but where is *Wonderland*? Why *Wonderland*? Is wonderland not part of the matrix?

Our life is ruled by our senses and the mind. We see something and we want it. We feel something and we desire her. We are indoctrinated with the concept of *sin*. Touch is a beautiful sense. Why would we feel guilty when we touch someone? Why would we feel shame when we have touched somebody?

It is the prophecy of the Oracle that the matrix will be destroyed. The strategy is the weaving of a Magic Carpet (in) Wonderland. The Magic Carpet will *eat up* the matrix and nothing of it will be left. The Magic Carpet will mystically unfold in all directions. You and I are stitching that Magic Carpet. Many people are involved. The real weavers are the libertines (the ones who are free), those who are unplugged or those who are born free in Zion.

The people who only operate with their senses and their mind are not free. You must learn to see outside of the mind. You must learn to feel by touch, without the mind. The task at hand is to become a no-mind. Nirvana is the great Peace. Only a no-mind is in peace. A mind is always at war and in conflict. It is surprising or indulging. It is making huge *spiritual* trips. Wild fantasies of an ego that will not pass through the magical Gate.

We have to learn how to become more peaceful. How? Not by demonstrating. We can only be in peace. Peace is our natural state. We have to learn to silence the mind. First we learn to de-identify. Before that we should contemplate about the colour blue and red. What is it that we really want? Tantra is actually only for people who do not desire 'tantra'. Those who are in it to experience *intimacy* and to be loved by many lovers are in it for the wrong reasons. Nothing is *wrong* of course, but the highest practice is not suitable for them. Tantra is for the vira.

Tantra involves touch. But it is a touch without preferences. It is a stitch. A stitch of the enfoldment of the Magic Carpet. A 'virus' of love. A liberating touch.

We see, we hear, we touch. Can there be something wrong with touch? Can seeing be wrong? When there is innocence? No contamination of *sin*? What is *the forbidden fruit*?

We do not only have the life with the mobile phone, SMS, internet, lovers, work, television, car, family, friends, music, food, sun, holidays, promotion, worries etc. There is something else. Something more. Don't you feel it? Do you sense it? How do you know that something is 'there' when you do not know *it* and cannot define 'it'?

Deep within man is the urge to know. If you asked people, nobody wants pain. Nobody wants fear. We all want to be fearless. Knowing is the same as fearlessness. How does this knowing come about? It comes about by inquiry. Does it only come about by inquiry? NO! In fact there is no causal relationship between these two even though I just seemingly said that. We inquire to lose the identity of the inquirer. That which is finite cannot know the infinite; the mind cannot enter Wonderland.

Somewhere we know that we are one. But it has to be fully experienced. This understanding does not come about by reading books. It is no use reading books by someone who read books of other folks and wrote down all their ideas in a book. It is no use visiting someone who visited many other people and now burdens interested listeners with intoxicating attractive ideas. This business of freeing a mind is very precise. One has to know exactly what one is doing, especially while using language!

There is a huge trap and a big mystery in language. Any word is potentially *dangerous.* Morpheus is very succinct in the way he uses language. It is very Twilight. Most people in the spiritual arena are fascinated by what gurus or excellent teachers say. It is, however, not what they say. It is the energy. It is a seduction. A seduction from the known to the unknown. *Dancing with a master* is dangerous. She will first want to undress you and then maybe kill you. But the dance continues. The beat goes on. The heart will go on. The breathing never stops.

Where, however, is my attention? Is the mind wandering off while I am touching? In dreams and fantasies? The wind touches my hair. Is that not sensual? My fingers touch the keyboard. Is that not sensual? What happens when the salt is thrown into the sea? Where is *the sin* when I am present? Why do you talk when I touch? You'd better shut up and be silent. Allow yourself to be touched. Shaktipata is descent of Divine Grace. In Kashmir Saivism this Shaktipata is the start of our spiritual endeavour.

The Shakti is the real liberator. Most of us are looking in the wrong place. We long to touch and to be touched. How about the touch of the *Divine*? This is what *Shaktipata* is and it is the start of our spiritual journey. Until we receive Shaktipata, most of our spiritual efforts are futile. You will understand this only after the Shaktipata. All is a matter of grace. Many of you need to do more thorough investigation into doer-ship. Virtually all of you think that *you* can 'achieve' 'liberation' by *your own efforts.* Neo could not unplug himself even with an IQ of 160. Yet, self-effort is everything.

Many readers are choosing the highway. Yoga, Beauty & Delight is not the highway. Many people make it very difficult. At the end the entire process is simple. But some people make it tough, holding on to the righteousness of the touchy-feely.

Especially when you are about to be touched.

Monk's Business

You must understand that these monks needed something to do. They could not just meditate, pray or chant all day. So they started to brew. They made beautiful wine and beer.

Watch the sky!

Keep looking.

Watch the Sky!

Tantra is indeed about the raising of our consciousness. To the highest summit and down. It is very precise. We want no accidents and therefore cannot accept 'muddling around'. You only need to add your devotion. In fact the devotion is already there, but you are so afraid to uncover it. Afraid to be hurt. You have not yet realised the power of devotion, otherwise you would be residing (t)here and drinking nectar.

Keep looking!

'Spirituality' is an insult if it is not carried on the wings of love. These wings are seeking you. They want to lift you up. You only need to let go and to surrender. Don't start to fantasize. The experiencing that I am talking about is deep relaxation and hard work. Self-realisation by niscam seva. Music will only be thoroughly enjoyed when it is made by a no-mind and enjoyed by a no-mind. That is where the real communion is. That is the celebration. You would be surprised to know the poem that Jimi Hendrix wrote on the evening of his death.

The guy was very aware and initiated. Like so many others. Like Bob Marley, the hero of the Rastafarians. A man I respect MUCH more than any present world leader you can mention.

Watch the Sky!

They would immediately understand that I am talking about the sky of the mind.

If 'the mind' is the earth, than what is the sky?

Some think that they are poor, but you are in fact all incredibly wealthy. And this wealth can easily be multiplied. What is it that you insist on keeping for yourself? Multiplication of wealth is what the great civilisations did, and I am writing nothing for nothing. If only your ears could be cleaned. If only you would learn to look a bit better and to really see and perceive.

Many official philosophers will not like my style and this philosophy because it is highly lucid and does not comply with their logic. In order to understand 'logic' we have to immerse ourselves in the opposite. You can determine by yourselves what that is. I have used the word often. We embrace the paradox. It has no structure and is hard to grasp. That is what many people do not like. There is no grip and they have to fall. This is not a mind-philosophy. It is a way to live. It is a lifestyle. But many of you cling to the morality of religion. It is known that Tantra is considered to be pagan. But why don't you look at the movie 'Mists of Avalon' or read that book and tell me about religion and these pagans. Pagan does not mean uncivilised. That is a big mistake. I am talking about lots of refinement and nobility. The nobility that I am inviting you into is not smeared with religious morality. That makes it too dangerous for most people. That is why I explained so often that Tantra is for the vira.

Tantra is also about ecstasy and delight. But unfortunately many people are afraid and full of doubt. It is strange for me. I do not understand the virus that some readers are caught up in. I say we can work miracles. The miracles start close-by. You need to realise who you are and what you are 'here' for. You need to hear the 'Calling' in your heart. Don't waste your time being interested. It is rare to have a human birth. And much more rare, to come into contact with such a truly divine philosophy and refined way of living.

It is not so difficult to see who is only here to steal and we will let them. It is not so hard to see who only wants to acquire and they may. It is easy to see who has lots of spiritual ambition and thinks themselves to be superior. They will explode sooner or later. Only a ripe fruit will fall. We are all struggling. That is OK. The Resistance requires you to be very steady, intelligent and aware. That is the entrance to join.

No use for talkers. Hypocrisy is murdered. There are heavy punishments for those who deceive and we are not the ones to hand out the punishment. You have to overcome all your fears in order to become who you are. You have to be a hero. You need to be brave and strong. We are talking about the opening of the heart and it is a blasting experience. If you do not prepare with love and devotion, you are not that able to take it. Some people have gone mad (insane).

But who is really insane? Are they more insane than you? What have you got to lose? Yes, you need to lose your sense of sanity. Your sanity is not leading to sameness. Let the Divine Madness arise in you. What is there to be afraid of? Do you really want it? Are you ready?

News

On this glorious day I have great news for you.
You are free! You are children of Zion.
Only one 'problem': we suffer a sort of amnesia.

But the other good news is that Grace is working in and for you. The inevitable is inescapable. Try to understand: Your mind is linked or plugged into the matrix. The matrix is all the mind-stuff and thought-forms.

Are you beginning to understand?

I hope that I am not writing all this for nothing.

....

So many people are still so much in the matrix ... It is really not necessary.

So many liberated souls have already shared their energy with you.

If you would only absorb it and take it in.

....

Really take it in!

Swallow the whole thing!

There are two worlds. But you only live in one of them.

In order to step into the other world, the mind needs to be unplugged. We can do it for you, but only when you prepare and are ready. When you are holding on much it becomes tough.

What is holding on? :

a. Strong identification with the persona and the body

b. Being stuck in all sorts of thoughts and feelings

c. Trying to secure your position with five different ships

d. Allowing your life to be shaped by others

e. Guru-shopping

f. Still being under heavy influence of the church, parents and others

g. Doubts, low self-esteem, fears etc. control your life

h. Believing yourself to be unworthy

i. Being greedy

j. Striving for fame, name, wealth, power and other illusions

k. Disloyalty to the Resistance or the Goddess (is this true?)

l. Being angry, revengeful and feeling hate or jealousy

m. Mainly focussing on achieving pleasures for yourself

n. Taking life (the obvious illusory side of it) too seriously

o. Thinking/believing that you can shape your destiny

p. Feeling superior to others

q. Trying to be scientific or rational

r. Being very concerned about how you look and come across to others!!!

s. Having strong concepts and ideas instead of being fluid

t. Feeling stuck in time and space instead of experiencing spaciousness

u. Judging things as 'wrong' or 'improper', especially in the 'spiritual arena'

v. Ridiculing others or gossip

w. Being afraid to look or behave foolish

x. Being rigid

y. Anything you hold to be sacred or holy

z. Religious and spiritual beliefs not empirically tested

aa. Afraid to give away

ab. (Rigidity in) sex and lovemaking

ac. Believing what the media and government tells you

ad. Giving power to certain symbols such as a cross

ae. Strong patterns of behaviour

af. Addictions

ag. Being afraid to use entheogens

ah. Afraid to love and/or to be loved

ai. Feeling the need to plan and to secure your future

aj. Not experimenting in sexual affairs

ak. Being prudish

al. Being highly moralistic

am. Insincere behaviours

an. Being attached to 'house' or 'car'

ao. Anything that is repressed

ap. All over-indulgent behaviour

aq. Showing off

ar. Believing that you are not creative

as. Thinking that others (who are showing off) are more advanced

at. Endlessly doing therapy and no niscam seva (selfless service)

au. Prolonging life unnaturally

av. Being afraid of death

aw. Any and all ignorance

ax. Any automatic behaviour and thinking

ay. Being afraid of 'hammering' instead of loving it

az. Sentimental love

ba. Trying to become 'realised' by relying on the mind

bb. Valuing pictures of the past

bc. Shame and guilt

bd. Being afraid of the devil or capital punishment

be. Thinking you need to become a child again

bf. Thinking that innocence (as a concept) is better than intelligence bg. Any and all thinking about this matter

bh. Believing that this is a good list

bi. Believing that if you let go of everything on this list you'll be better off

bj. Liking do's and don't s instead of becoming a big boy or girl

bk. Having fantasies about the monastic life

bl. Flirting with Tantra while staying loyal to the lies, corruption, dreams, threats, fantasies and hypocrisy of organised religion

bm. Hoping that Morpheus will 'save' you

bn. Irritation about this text

bo. Cowardish traits

bp. Investing money in the matrix world to increase your personal 'wealth'

bq. Having (too many) insurances and pension-plans

br. Dogmatic ideas about meat and vegetarians

bs. Greed (2nd mentioning ...)

bt. Any idea that affirms duality

bu. Defending yourself

bv. Playing with me in the matrix in an unfair and dishonest way.

bw. of course very important: NARROW-MINDEDNESS!

What if it is your choice to be unplugged or to hold on?

Lionheart @ Crossroads

Your mind does not yet have the faith to go under. Logically, that is. But, my friend, your heart knows. Always trust the heart! The practice of Tantra will bring you to the place where there is no fear. When all doubts are vaporised, what remains is trust.

Tantra is a huge and precious gift for millions of people.
There are very intensive processes in the practice of Tantra whereby the practitioner destroys all he is and then builds up a new body with totally different energy.

That is why the right guidance is very important.

Surrender is one of the things by which you move from being a candidate for Tantra to being a practitioner of Tantra (sort of 'student' and 'disciple' although that is slightly different).

A thinker does thinking.

An experiencer is experiencing.

Through a master happens mastering!

Most people who approach me say that they are interested in this path, and when I ask why, they say that they want to work on some limitations or such. That. however, is the domain of personal growth only. In that domain we replace one thing with another. Tantra is much more radical and dangerous.

I have explained that one can only really 'learn' (discover) the depth of Tantra through being with a guru or master. Nobody is a master for everybody. JC was a master only for some people, and most people considered him to be a crook. During his life only one of his disciples became a master. It is not at all rare that many good disciples reach mastery after the physical death of the master.

But still it is a mystery what and who the master is. I often talk about the guru-principle. I am Ralph. I have a physical body and I have, let's say, an astral or energetic body. The master is not so much the physio/psychological complex, but it is sort of the energy that that person has built up and is carrying (wanting to spread).

That energy is Tantra. The energy wants to spread. But it is difficult to bear this energy (Kundalini-Shakti) because it is very powerful. That is why we often talk about kundalini as the snake. Not many people will be able to hold the snake. And the snake is travelling through a small hollow bamboo (your nervous system). Only when it sticks its neck out over the top of the bamboo (Sahasrara), will it not fall back again. Before that – no matter how well things are going – there is always a possibility of a downfall.

Most of the disciples of JC received the revelations after the death of JC. Their time with JC was however very important. That is where the energy was built up, even though they didn't understand a thing of his teachings and did not recognise the process. I have so often explained that a mind cannot understand a no-mind. NEVER! This is according to the very important principle of Shaktipata. Shaktipata is the most important thing for our progress in non-dualistic Kashmir Saivism. It is one of the things that sets Kashmir Saivism totally apart from other approaches.

A master of course wants to make other masters. That is very understandable and highly logical. Only impostors always desire to have authority over others and like people to be dependent on them. Only an ego desires 'power' and control. BUT; the process of mastering is very intense. In Tantra we have to be willing to destroy (let go of) everything. This goes MUCH MORE deep than you can imagine right now. It is very fierce.

It is very rare for someone to do that process on his or her own. Very rare indeed. Virtually all great realised souls had the guidance of someone who trod the difficult road before. Some of them have been so nice as to leave certain signposts or pointers for us. They left invisible footprints for us to follow. Maybe we all are a master somewhere and somehow, but still some 'mastering' is necessary (amnesia). There are deep tendencies and impressions to let go off. Some of the conditioning is very profound. In Kashmir Saivism there are also very important initiations or energy-transfers. This is made very clear in the movie the Matrix.

The Matrix shows that there is 'unplugging' and there is a training program with the use of certain computer programs, which are downloaded (initiations and 'upgrades').

In most schools one first has to learn to become empty and to unload. Then there are – maybe – certain initiations. In Kashmir Saivism we start with the Shaktipata as that makes the process of de-conditioning much easier. De-conditioning is cutting through the illusion in which we are seemingly caught. Unplugging means we let go of everything; and this word 'everything' may encompass more than you can imagine. That is why you need to have faith and be willing to let go and especially to surrender.

When the surrender is not strong, you will run away from your master. Most people don't make it longer than six months. If someone is very ready, a good master can unplug them quickly, as happens in the movie the Matrix. But this is rare. VERY rare! It is possible however. But only when the student is very apt, determined, aware, lucid (unstructured) and has lots of faith, commitment and surrender.

In the movie The Mists of Avalon – which I highly recommend anyone seeing, who is seriously considering whether to pursue the path of mysticism in the pagan tantric tradition – several things are made very clear. Arthur received a very strong training program in mysticism in the School of the Goddess, as it existed in England in the early ages. It was the time before Christianity destroyed many beautiful things. It took several years full time with an excellent druid and master like Merlin. Still he received his full communication with the Goddess after he completed training school and in fact – and this is remarkable – after the death of his father. 'Father' also hints at guru in some cases.

What I am talking about is a total initiation in the mystery school. It is not for everyone. It is in fact for a few very brave, loving, caring and heroic souls. The training happens in a totally unpredictable and mysterious way. There is not much I will say about it in advance. You cannot do it while deciding to hold on to any idea, thought, moral or rule. I want to make this clear now.

It is very important that you inquire into what Tantra is for you, and then you must also be willing to let go of the ideas that you have about what it is and what it is not, as it is very different to what you are probably capable of thinking it is. Also you have to investigate your ideas of what and who a master is and how this person should or should not behave. Use this while selecting your master but during the anchoring you need to let go of everything. 'The master' will totally change! A tantric master will not look like what you romanticise he is. He will lead you to experiencing and drinking.

I am not here to tell you whether or not 'demons', goblins, ghosts and spirits exist. We tell you to have dinner in the graveyard and to see for yourself!

You have to go within. That is where the entire training program takes place. Most people haven't even seen that aspect of the movie the Matrix yet. Part of the practice is that you tune in to the master. That is however not the person or the physical body of the guru, but the 'special energy', so to say. That energy is Shiva; that is when you 'perceive' (realise/attain) it non-dually. That energy in a more kinetic form (still 'invisible') lies asleep at the base of your spine.

Tantra is the kundalini-sadhana. For that very strong and difficult sadhana you have to train yourself to become very aware, very disciplined, strong and authentic. Honesty with the master is inevitable. That person will get to know you inside and out. Your only rescue is honesty. Otherwise you will make a total fool and idiot of yourself. This path requires lots of intelligence. I am talking about an intelligence that even many seemingly intelligent people do not have. It is an intelligence and wakefulness that will totally and entirely unplug you from the matrix-world.

Tantra is not only about 'knowledge'. Maybe this sounds like a strange sentence to you, but many exceptionally highly developed systems of thinking and philosophy describe 'knowledge' as their goal. Maybe you should understand Tantra as 'pure knowledge' or as wisdom. It is the esoteric knowledge of how to be free from the mind and thus to be liberated from ignorance. This is the Truth that Morpheus also talks about. It is the liberation from the matrix. But in Tantra we emphasise true and total liberation from any and all elements in the matrix (illusory world). That is why the practice of Tantra goes very deep, far and extreme. More 'extreme' (far) than any other system I know of.

You really need to be prepared for shocks and 'disgusting' revelations. It is certainly not only a joyful process. You will feel deep fears, your heart will be torn, your soul will be ripped open and your personality will be smashed. But only in as much as it is possible with you. That means that you need to do all the preparatory work. This non-dual Tantra philosophy is really only for highly 'advanced' students. And I am sorry; I truly do not mean this in 'exclusive' or elitist terms at all. I mean most ready. Very aware. You must basically be ready to be unplugged.

That means that if you want to study with us, it must really be like you enter a monastery. All the same rules and things apply, only I am not asking you to give up your matrix life. The renunciation is of the mind and all the mental conditioning. You must have the same dedication.

I like to see you all inspired. INSPIRED is much more preferable than sleeping. So many things are possible, but there is too much tamas (inertia, dullness, sleep, unwakefulness). Your master can help you to destroy the tamasic tendencies in your personality/being.

But you must give permission. You must work to become more awake, alert, wakeful and disciplined. Tantra is in fact freedom, but you can only acquire total freedom by exercising extreme discipline. Why? The mind is very slippery and it will trick and fool you. It will fool you into thinking that you are very 'spiritual' and 'enlightened' already while you are merely a machine. A virus according to agent Smith.

And it is this machine and virus that I am trying to establish communication with and try to get a commitment from. This machine needs to work its way out of the mind and into contacting the soul and Spirit. We need mind over body and soul over mind. That is why you have to also practise right discrimination. The ultimate realisation will be shocking even though many things will go very gradually. Almost unnoticed. But when you look back a year it is (at least it can be) huge. That is the beauty of Tantra. It goes VERY fast and deep and it is very profound. Shocking and gradual. There is a safety net but it is also dangerous.

In Tantra people strive not only for knowledge, as I described before, but also for power. (In most philosophies they do not.) But, strangely, this 'power' is not an ego-power. This is what makes it very delicate. The entire process is rather subtle. You will become free, full of love AND very powerful. These people used to be called witches and many other names. Many of them were killed. They needed to hide. In alchemical laboratories e.g. in caves high in the snow and ice of the Himalayas.

This mysticism is offering a hand to you. Most of your hands are oily, greasy and wet with sweat. They are not strong enough. Only a King (Arthur) can draw the sword. Are you that king? Are you Neo? Is your heart totally pledged? Are you very sure and without 'Cypher-tendencies'? Because they will die an ugly death with us. The quest of this work is to raise Conquerors and nothing less. The world especially needs female saints. Are you willing to enter the world of magic and witchcraft? If you only want right self-knowledge, then I invite you to come with me, pure hearts.

But you may have to be willing to experience some 'nasty things' as well, as Frodo had to in Lord of the Rings. Who is to become Lord of the Ring?

And try to imagine that a master is not someone who is perfect, although He or She is in a certain way. A master is someone through whom the master-energy flows (the Christ-consciousness). Jesus is the guy and Jesus Christ is the full manifestation of the Shakti-energy in a person.

Certain 'traits' are important. The willingness to give, the willingness to suffer and to sacrifice, a strong sense of niscam seva, will-power, loyalty, devotion and surrender. When this is all present, nothing can go wrong. That is why we say Tantra is for the vira.

Mysticism is built up from within. It requires you to be more in nature, by yourself and in silence. Mysticism does not seek a talking mind. At first, in any monastery, you have to learn to talk less, and also to talk less about yourself. You must in a way lose your self-importance.

And then some One can understand and appreciate the teachings of Mirdad. The Book of Mirdad will for most people be a collection of nice and beautiful sounding words. For others it will be a huge and powerful revelation. For others it will be a wine of a great vintage leaving you 'spell-bound'.

Iron, Brain and Void

How does a piece of metal become a magnet? What makes one magnet more powerful than another? This is the 'power' that we are talking about in Tantra. The alchemy of turning an ordinary piece of metal into a magnet. A magnet has to be very aware of whose vicinity 'it' is in. Otherwise it may draw in unwanted energies.

Tantra is all about energy.

Tantra is the raising (expanding) of consciousness. It is still a mystery how it happens. People have used terms such as 'the mind', 'the over-mind', 'the super-mind', 'the unconscious mind', 'the superconscious', and 'the supramental'. We can surely impress readers with many words.

In the old days people died by a stone, an animal, a real accident, a serious disease, a bullet or a sword. These days people are already dead before the battle has even begun. They mostly faint by words. Words have the effect of bullets. They wear some people down.

Paravak is the state beyond any word, form or symbol. We have to use symbols and words to go beyond them. Only then will we know Truth. The Truth-consciousness (devoid of morals, ideas and concepts) manifests in our head/brain as truth. In our heart it manifests as love. In our body it manifests as peace. In our environment it shows up as Oneness (it is 4 u to figure out how Divine Madness arises). That is when there is nothing in-between anymore. This Oneness only shows up when the Truth has descended into our entire being. When our tongue has been purified of ignorance and lies. When our heart has been cleansed of hate and jealousy. When our body has been cleared of stress and impurities.

Therefore we have to enter the void. The great void is the unknown. You have to realise the sameness, and not in a cerebral or intellectual way. Investigate your brain: All these thoughts and processes are supposed to be happening in your brain. But what is the brain? When we take the entire void out of it, all the 'matter' of your brain is condensed into a teeny-weeny speck of dust that you are not even able to see with the eye. That is what the brain is. It is just a very intelligent sort of 'thinking void'.

Now, what about the galaxy? Can it be the same? Can it be that all these stars and the void are actually intelligent? When all the matter of the planet earth is condensed, they say it is the size of a ping-pong ball. It is not that certain that *any* matter exists. Certainly there are waves. These waves seem to be changing into particles sometimes, but we are not sure, because when we are not observing them, they disappear.

I mean this is just a very lucid and totally mysterious place! The light of the sun travels a few light minutes to reach our eye, but the light of the moon (which is a reflection) takes much less than a light second. And the moon very much shapes the surface of the earth. It exercises powers of 'magnetism'. It has controlled the tides for aeons of time already. At first there was only a vast ocean on the surface of the planet. Certain forces shaped the destiny of the earth. Amoebas (single-celled beings) crawled out of the sea and through evolution turned into man.

Still miraculous processes take place when a man fertilizes a woman. Out of these millions of sperm cells, one is gonna make it. And it splits and divides. But among all the divisions there is wholeness. There is consciousness. Even an amoeba has consciousness. Scientific tests show that even this tiny one-celled 'thing' can be conditioned in a certain way. Intelligence is everywhere. This is a 'thinking' universe. Human beings are not the only ones. There is a high chance that there are other life forms in this vast galaxy. Maybe the entire galaxy is very intelligent.

If suddenly everything on planet earth, including the earth itself, became half the size would you notice?

Would anyone notice?

What does this tell you?

If time and all speeds suddenly went twice as fast, how would anyone know?

Are you getting any idea about the magic of all of this?

It is much 'stranger' than you think.

In order to come to full realisation we need to use our fantasy beyond imagination. Our intuition beyond time - and space sensing. We have to fly to new frontiers. We have to dive and be willing to drown. We have to learn to look without glasses, spectacles, ideas, thought-forms, morals and judgements. We have to learn to listen to the great Silence deep within the recesses of our heart. We need to investigate the spacious Space and realise it to be the same. We have to practise holding our head up high and bending.

Are you a piece of iron, a magnet or gold? Do you care about money or about becoming a jewel?

Most people are rotten on the inside. They put on fancy clothes, make-up and expensive scents. They behave with conditioned manners. They donate money to silly organisations who just squander it trying to hide and seal the disastrous effects of our ridiculous way of life. And yet – somewhere in this pool of mud – great diamonds are hidden. The most beautiful of all flowers grows out of the mud. The rose protects itself with thorns. Beneath the wings of love is hidden a dagger.

Are you afraid of blood?

All your blood will become crystalline. That is how it goes on Mt. Kailash. But the lid has to be opened. What is in must come out. What do you store deep down inside? Why do you try to prevent your chest from being ripped open? Is there something afraid of seeing the light? We must set 'it' free in order for you to experience freedom. During the day you may try to behave, but why do you have vivid dreams at night?

In Tantra you need the courage to make love with the beast. The beast does not accept society's conditioning tricks. In the city you may survive, but in the jungle there is only one law. Trees all grow in the same way. You may be fascinated by the leaves and branches, but I am talking about the roots. As above, so below. It is a vast network of branches. Only the trunk of the tree is alone; its branches and boughs are all intermingled with great delicacy and delight.

All of nature is making love, but many people predominantly think about sex. Its energy is so dangerous that it drives you to insanity.

Why do you identify so proudly with the trunk alone? Are you afraid of growing a sharp thorn? Are you afraid to go underground because that is the domain of the Resistance? The branches do the intelligent work of passing nourishing liquids to the entire organism. When you set out to go Deep-Soul-Diving, you have to go very deep. You have to push the frontiers. The first drop of nectar (usually) takes many years to squeeze.

In most eastern traditions you need to do many years of intensive sadhana before the master really starts to work with you. You have to prepare yourself. One needs to prepare very well in order to receive the shock. You have to become very steady and one-pointed. You have to acquire lots of mastery in order to carry the energy of mastery. It is a slight change that makes a huge difference. When you are impatient, you'll have to wait a lot longer. When you are (spiritually) ambitious, you will be handed a great illusion.

It is a matter of utmost awareness and alertness. Do you like to work for a living and are you trying hard to 'make it', or do you have a strong inclination for niscam seva? You need to figure out why you are here. What is here is everywhere. 'Where' are you? Your life may be very important. And it is! You certainly have strong responsibilities.

There is a much better life for you 'in store'. It is in fact outside of the store in which you are currently shopping and residing. The only thing we are asking of you is willingness to die to the old life that you have been living. That question of course makes you very afraid. You treasure your life very much. How important is one of your dreams at night? Will you refuse to wake up because it is such a nice dream? Only if you are a very sentimental person and you insist on living in your emotional dramas.

So what are you vigorously holding on to? You nearly know what life is, but certainly want to stay a piece of metal for the rest of your life.... Why don't you try some magnetism? You must know somewhere that a touch of magic is inevitable. Do you prefer mass hysteria to the intelligence of quiet alchemists? Many people go to Spain to lie on the beach during vacation, but some people like to wander in the mountains. It is not impossible that when you are very thirsty, you will find a beautiful stream of Living Water. When you drink, this stream widens and more pure wisdom flows. It has always been there for you, beloved.

Treading the Path of Mysticism

We may be well on the way of walking the Path of Mysticism when we experience:

- more problems and challenges in life AND more 'flow' and inner guidance.
- strong relationship turbulence AND much deeper love for many people.
- more confusion AND much stronger clarity and inner wisdom.

All these experiences show that our surrender can be more, deeper and more intense, but we have some attachment to 'struggling'.

Some of us feel that we would like to perform some daily rituals to show and shower forth our devotion. Great rituals can be performed from dense ignorance. It all depends on our attitude / level of awareness. For a saint, every act is a ritual. Every step is a step with awareness on Mother Earth. Every gesture can be a piece of art. A ritual performed with the mind, will only deepen the mind-rut. A mind is only rattling in meditation and a no-mind is meditating all the time. A mind misinterprets every word and act of a great master and a no-mind just rejoices in love.

Science, my friends, is the opposite of 'tradition'. Mysticism is not scientific. Science is created by the intellect and its offshoot is technology. A scientific mind cannot bridge the two worlds. Science deals with the realm that can be seen by the senses. It is rational and logical. Things can be measured. There is cause and effect. Things are predictable. Tradition passes on 'another realm' that cannot be perceived with the gross senses. Mysticism will never come to meet science. Scientists are desperately trying to approach mysticism, but they are chasing the rainbow's end. A more intelligent leap is necessary.

Struggling is not un-useful, but we cannot struggle our way into heaven. We must learn to juggle. Struggling strongly involves the ego. We have to fall (let go) and to submit. Human beings need to discover the beauty of surrender. We stay intelligent, but we develop a much higher form of intelligence. An intelligence, which is not based on separation, but on wholeness. It is based on, brings forth, showers and shows wholeness. It is derived from wholeness and is whole and holy. This is the Holy Insight that prophets like Mirdad try to pass on.

Many people, however, prefer their own insight. It is clouded in misperceptions and ignorance. The mind of man experiences guilt unto the bitter end. 'Guilt' is an outward projection of the ego as it tries to hide a treasure from us. All we need to do is to watch the mind (keep looking). We cannot heal ourselves because we are looking from a wound, with a wound, into a wound. All that we perceive is veils.

Only when we let go of our ideas of what is logical and rational, only when we penetrate through the essence of our fears does the great secret unveil Itself and then the two worlds meet. We are on the threshold of creation. Two oceans merge into a mighty stream and we are washed totally clean and come out refreshed and anew. That is when we develop the heroism to really find out what 'mysticism' is and we realise that we will never know. We laughingly embrace the mighty Unknown.

We allow ourselves to become a force of mysticism, because we realise the dynamic thrill of it all. We abide in the Great Understanding that no sin exists in pleasure for she who is established in yoga (unity). There is nothing to reject, as nothing is the cornerstone of Everything. We let go of the need to explain and convince others (in a rational way) and just share great works of art and poetry. On the Path of Yoga, Beauty & Delight we are lovers and not explainers/convincers. People do not like to change their mind, but they do love to (make) love.

The revolution that I describe is a powerful revolution. It is a revolution with, from and through love. It is a revolution that will bring about anarchy. It is the experience of the joy of becoming empty and not striving anymore for personal gain. Once we let go of the need to protect, we can share freely. And what else is there to share? Would you want to share your superiority or prefer to be slain? A mind is very impressive, but can never beat love. A great scientist can be fairly intelligent, but a Conqueror demonstrates the will power, intelligence and surrender to subdue the automaton. There is no other battle.

In the Resistance we are conquerors of hearts. Weaving the Magical Carpet requires no plan. The Americans spend billions of dollars chasing a few men. Such a war is never won. Mankind has known many wars. God bless the poor souls who call them 'holy'. Every automaton is a terrorist. I am all for killing all the terrorists. But let us be brave and intelligent. We can learn our lessons from history especially when we understand Stephen Hawking's 'Brief history of time'.

There is great evolution in machines. Some machines can do a better job than many an automaton. What is the future of the human race? Where is our intelligence leading us? All the intelligent people should strive much harder to become much more intelligent. I am talking about a higher intelligence which is very distinct from the usual mind-stuff. The mind-stuff has no power to liberate. Not even to see clearly.

Hear how Mirdad longs to suck the poison out of you. He longs to lift the lid on your heart. But what do you do?

We need a master! We need soul over mind. You are in desperate need of a higher intelligence. Discern that your weakness is looking for more sentiment. I refuse to give it to you. Of course I love to dance with you, but only when you are drunk. Drink the wine that will ease up the rigidity of your mind. The fortress needs to be besieged. It will happen in a different way to how you imagine anyway, so why do you try to think about it so much? I am just offering you a good drink. I have no plans for making love. I have not learned to count. I am not quantifying nor qualifying so why are you?

My dear friends, dress beautifully even when you go to a funeral. Keep your head up to the sky. Keep looking. Become ready for love and watch the borders disappear. Sail purposefully into the mist and beware of the Miracle. Direct your attention towards Shiva and know that He is the Lord of mysticism and symbols. All will become clear at one point. Allow your mind to vaporise. Start to feel the lucidity in what is real. Do not be afraid to go nuts. It cannot get worse than it is. Can it? Can it get any worse? Hardly. Isn't that so? So have some faith my friend. Moral people with lots of stories and explanations carry a heavy load. Throw away that load and float! Why are you so burdened?

I offer you a flame and what is it that you decide to burn in it? What is your heart's desire? We seemingly can create and destroy. When your powers are rising you have to be very sure of what to create and what to destroy. Make a pledge in your heart.

The ship is ready.

The daughter of the Ocean is awaiting.

Wisdom

How does wisdom arise, friends?

Is it out of books?

From life's experiences?

By the words of our guru or master?

No!

Wisdom comes from within. It is a fountainhead and you need to find access to this inner well.

As I wrote before, it is a matter of sruti and smriti; remembering and forgetting. Most of us carry something from our previous lives. But unfortunately we do not have access to it. We forgot.

In order to gain access we have to become very relaxed. We need to have deep meditation experiences. We need trance (lucid) states of consciousness. The magic is all around us, but we do not see it.

Several friends of mine are going through severe difficulties in life and yet they are grateful. They experience an inner power rising.

Spirituality is very surprising. We strive and strain. We struggle and we fall. Finally we surrender. It is only THEN that we start to hear. It is only then that our eyes begin to open. Before, we read about spirituality. Now we know something about it.

I have said so often that Tantra has to be experienced. Yet most of us are only collecting ideas. To get any closer we have to de-condition, or allow this process to happen. Many people who are reading this book or who attend a bit of my work are really not ready for Tantra at all. Most of us are much better at 'holding on to' than 'letting go'. We especially hold on to insanity (we think we are very sane) and are afraid to let go of the mind.

There is the path of morals and there is the path of liberty. All those who are puritans, had better think twice about what they are holding in place. I would rather that you became more mature and investigated the source of your guilt and fear. Why are you a talker instead of a practitioner?

If we look around the world we can see that we are in a lot of turmoil. I suppose that you have acquired some wisdom by now to understand that it is because we as human beings have a lot of fear, jealousy and hate in our hearts. Tantra likes to push it out. Gurus and masters are supposed to 'help' in that. But it is very nice when the candidates aspire to be at least some sort of a hero, and are willing to work through all these emotions. It is OK that they surface. That is the whole idea. But in which direction are they going? The coward energises these false emotions and allows them to live a life by themselves. That means they get projected outward into a gigantic matrix. The hero internalises and inquires. She inquires so long and so deeply that the illusion vaporises. There is only fear and love, and upon deep inquiry there is only love.

This is the teaching of Tantra. We like to live in love, but many people seem to prefer to live amidst war. I have emphasised that the whole thing is very delicate. As soon as there is a strong energy to live Tantra, apparently some other energies also swirl in. We have to be very clear and steady and unfortunately many people are not (yet). Destruction comes from inside. It comes from our midst.

If you have a problem with drugs, sex or group-sex, you can do two things. You can bail out or investigate what gives rise to your resistance. I don't like it when people read Shakespeare, Hafiz or Rumi and really like it, and at the same time get agitated with the use of drugs or liberal sex. It is nice when you marvel at the works of Gaudi, but at least try to become a Gaudi. The obviousness of the magic mushrooms is all over. But most people are muddlers and fiddlers. There is something – maybe – with a magic mushroom. But it is not merely the magic mushroom, my friend.

The mushroom creates an opening, but much more important than the substance is the energy in which you are working. Many people engage in group-sex. That is not Tantra. Tantra does involve rituals and an outsider could perceive some as an orgy. Tantra is for the vira. It is certainly not bhoga, although we do not denounce pleasure. Pleasure is used as a spiritual practice. And why not?

I have explained that Tantra is dangerous. Especially in 'my' school I want people to be very clear. I have written hundreds of pages already on a very lucid and dazzling philosophy. There is also a practice. That practice may consist of meditation, self-inquiry, silence, dance, 3-D listening, confrontation, exhaustion, unloading, expansion, de-conditioning etc. We can also learn to meditate while making love. Lovemaking is the most (at least one of the most) spiritual experience(s) on earth. In fact it helps us to transcend the earthly, bodily realm and to enter heaven. Mystic initiations are part of Tantra.

In several pyramids they found traces of the blue lotus. This is a strong entheogen. But the people were very well prepared. In and around these pyramids, many priests and priestesses were prepared for many years. After many years of arduous work, some of them received the mystic initiation.

By yourself you can have group-sex, but that has nothing to do with Tantra. Only an initiate can raise the energy to make it into a tantric experience. That requires the invocation of a sort of an 'overmind'. All the participants must be very well aligned. There is a strong protocol. Usually the pujari decides with whom you will make love (unite; yoga) that night. That person becomes your Shiva or Shakti, but only for that night. On that night only you are married with that person. You are not to associate, write or talk with that person outside of the ritual. The ritual is a sacred act. You should not develop any identifications with that person after the ritual.

The rituals often take place on new moon or full moon and in a secret place. It is by invitation. The purpose of the ritual is expansion (tantra). It is to spread (love). We have to escape the limitations of the mind that identifies with a body as 'his' or 'her' own. It happens from a place of sacredness. The body is our temple. When the overmind sets in, some sense of yoga is starting to happen. Making love with another person helps us to go beyond the ordinary boundaries. Making love with this Shakti is making love with the entire universe and helps us to realise that the Shakti is in every (wo)man. Making love with this Shiva is making love with the universal and mythological Shiva.

Because the overmind is present, the experience of pleasure and delight is stronger. When the Shaktis open up to the experience of delight, they (may) start to experience the flow of kundalini. By luck or Grace it is possible that some men get initiated and also experience an opening up and access their feminine side. This leads to the experience of wholeness. The way to Shiva is through Shakti. That is why in Tantra women are revered.

In this ritual men adore their Shakti. It is worshipping the divine. Why not worship the divine through and with (in) pleasure and delight? When the heart is pure and the awareness is raised, it is a ritual invoking the presence of the Goddess. When the people are not prepared enough, it is an orgy (emphasis on bhoga). No jealousy is 'allowed'. The participants are joined together in destiny. It is very important that the entire ritual is performed in a certain way as outlined by the pujari. Mostly such a ritual involves the five M's. This is all part of the left-hand path of courage.

Jealousy may surface, but it is (better to be) worked through by the group, before entering into the heavy practices of Tantra.

And why these practices? Strangely enough they lead to the deepest and most encompassing wisdom, which is the domain of the Great Goddess. This is Her Gift to humanity.

Worship

There is only one way to really worship Shiva and that is to become Shiva. The best way to worship Shakti is to become Shakti.

Once people have become excellent scholars, the tantric sadhana invites all to apply and practise. It is with vigour, love and joy. This movement is alive. There is nothing that is denied. Kashmiri Saivists enjoy sensuous pleasures; we dance and make music with drums.

All the senses are involved. There is no room for the theory of illusion. It is a joyous affirmation of the world. Not based on gathering possessions, but on giving and sharing freely.

On the path of Yoga Beauty & Delight we joyously act. We create. Make love. Write great poetry. Paint a beautiful painting. Enjoy the works and art of others. Dance; but dance in ecstasy. The Nataraja points with his fourth arm (hand) towards his raised foot indicating total and joyous liberation.

This interaction can only be with and in the heart. Therefore our heart needs to expand. This is the expansion of love. We embrace the world. Lovingly and joyfully. Be involved in the world. Use the time, resources and energy that you have, not to gather and to accumulate, but to unload, to help, to share and to give. This is what life is about and we all know it.

I wish you to hear with two ears strung together becoming one ear: the third ear! I wish you to see with two eyes melted by mysticism into one: the third eye. It is only there and then that we can really commune and interact.

Is it important to you to hang on to the small individuality with all its concerns, worries and judgements? Or are you ready to offer it into the fire of love? Is your heart ploughed to carry some precious seeds? Because this is the way that Tantra will spread as Tantra. It is not by books, lectures or idle talk. The world has enough (of its) philosophers. We need men and women who apply and life 200% of life. Let's apply ourselves and make it work.

Who knows how many years the earth still has. Who knows how many years you still have. This time is crucial. The world is in desperate need of masters. A master is not a parrot. A master is not a slave. A master is not a mule. A master is not merely a brilliant mind. A master is not an arrogant person or a bitch. A master is not predictable. A master is not into wealth or abundance. She cares not for fame, name or status. A master is simply an exponent of the Truth with no concessions (like Osho, JC, Morpheus, Socrates, Hafiz and so many others). It is not difficult my friends. All the ideas make it difficult. So difficult that the recognition is deformed.

A master is a totally modern man or woman. She is a revolutionary and causes a revolution. It is (maybe) not even intended. A master is a simple man. He is not an arrogant person. He or she does not care or worry about him or herself. Start with the proper worship dear brothers and sisters. Long to be an instrument making beautiful music in a glorious symphony. Are you afraid to shake or to tremble? Do you not dare to vibrate? When you decide to be stagnant or rigid all is lost. Introduce fluidity. Tantra is not bourgeois. Start to throw away your boring wardrobe and buy some new, fresh and colourful clothes. There is plenty in store.

It is only your framework that prevents you from blossoming. Be free and go wild.
Be willing to look and be a total fool.

Touch II

I have written about this heavily charged subject – 'Touch' – before.

Who minds having an orgasm?

Who does not like to be exquisitely and lovingly touched?

All the earth, animals, rocks and trees are naked. Why do we insist on being dressed up in front of each other?

What is the danger in meeting nakedly?

What is so important to hide?
Is an orgasm, in fact, in the mind or in the body? Or is it both? Can it be an out-of mind/body experience? What a beautiful I-land that will be ...

Be very aware of who you hang out with. Everything is an exchange of energy. Most of us are infantile and underdeveloped in recognizing energies. We recognise very late. Now is the time to prepare a fertile ground so that tantric seeds can grow inside of you. Prepare for a very precious flower to blossom. Make yourself receptive to receive a divine flame.

You sow with all your words and actions. There is always a transmission of energy. Everything is energy. Profound understanding is very necessary. This requires even more awareness. Much deeper relaxation. Much more surrender. Much better absorption.

What if love does not accept being channelled through your mind's rules of what 'love' is and is not? Maybe love is something very much different to what you think and hold it to be. Is that possible? What if love is free flowing? Then we will never be able to catch Her with our mind and its rules. Maybe real love has nothing to do with our 'loving' thoughts and 'loving' behaviours, which more often than not prove to be childish and conditional. There is still a lot of 'if ... then' even with very spiritual people.

Who is willing to give a lecture to us about the real meaning of love? Do you really know? I am sure that you have felt loved. Hopefully you feel loved. Right now. Is love for only one person real love?

I am not saying that it is not. It is very beautiful. This nobility, pureness and loyalty is beautiful. But mostly I see a monster that is dressed up. I can see through your clothes. What I see then is soo beautiful. I see monsters and beasts. I see very strange movements of a love that is unable to flow and express. I see the longing. I see the pain of separation.

We cuddle a horse, a cat or a dog. We don't worry about its gender. Won't it be great when we can just express our love and attraction? Our desires? How will it be when you do not have to be afraid or ashamed of what you want? When you do not have to hide your secret longings and wishes? Look at society! Are the 'happy' couples really happy? Why are there all the naked women in magazines? Why is there so much repression and oppression?

Why are certain things OK and others not? I like to explore these boundaries. Do you also want and long to grow in love and consciousness? Kissing each other on the cheek is fine. One kiss on the lips is often OK. Hugging is good and healthy. What about a very long hug? What about when you feel something in your hips and pelvic area? Must you then move away to someone/-where else? Putting an arm around someone is OK isn't it? But when does it go too far for you?

Are you trying to tell me that all of society is so great and that 'this' is dangerous? You must be very astute to try to convince or persuade me ...

Are you with a partner? What is accepted by your partner and what is not? What are your agreements? Do you like these agreements? Do they make you both most happy? Is nothing suppressed? Are you OK when your partner shares love with another? Until how far? Are they allowed to write emails to other people? Massage the back of another? The feet but not the belly? Where is the exact line? Can you draw it on my body? What if I like you to go a little bit lower? That area is just sooo sensuous to me. I really like it when you touch me there very softly. I like you to cross the line.

How else to expand? How else to discover what is there when you refuse to live the rest of your life in a self-imposed prison?

And now what do we have when you cross the line in touching 'another'?

Is this love?

Where is the control? Who is in control?

Do you like the society that we live in?

It is the society that we live in, but do you like it? Of course you 'accept' it, but can it be different? Better?

How does childish love mature? Will it ever mature in this civilisation?

Why do people living together have so many fights?

Where does the lock or the lid come from? Who put it on and who keeps it in place? Where is the master-key? Is the lock or the lid less love than the content or the master-key?

In Tantra we offer an alternative. It requires a lot of common sense. It is highly practical. It is very advanced and it is in fact also intelligent. What we have now is sort of animalistic. It is based on 'possession' is n't it? People are possessed and they like to possess. Something or someone that is free cannot be possessed. We can share. Rejoice. Multiply. Spread. I prefer you to be tender rather than being so rigid about gender.

Does your gender control your mind? In most people it does. It is killing. It drives people insane. Better to let the tension out. Explore it. Don't judge too much. What have all your judgements and opinions helped or relieved? Ease up a bit. Grow into much higher intelligence (buddhi → overmind). Don't be so tight and rigid. Loosen your belt. Let some air in. Breathe and become more spacious. Real love is very spacious. Love is expansion. It is movement. Spanda. There is a contraction and expansion. Research consciousness. Tantra is research in consciousness. It is not stirring the mind (only).

When you have hardly been a day alone in your life without TV, radio, phone and email; not seeing anyone, what have you to say about these yogis? There is not much that has been discovered in science in the west that they were not aware of. Touch is a supreme sense, unfortunately religiously underdeveloped.

Allow yourself to be touched. Feel the serenity. Surrender in the touch and let go. LET GO. Relax. Don't be so tense. How can you deepen lovemaking with all this tension? Learn to relax much more and much deeper. If only you could be totally relaxed. Even when you think you are totally relaxed you still hold a lot of tension. In the jaw. In your anus. In the back and in your feet. In so many places. Take a good deep tissue massage. Touch and be touched. Explore. This is an exploration journey. But when you do not want to go five meters to the left or the right, there is not much to 'explore'.

Vigilant Awareness

One of the most important things for students in the Path of Yoga, Beauty & Delight to develop is vigilant awareness (avadhna). I have often asked my students to make a superhuman effort to be aware during the programs that I conduct. Of course each person tries to do as well as they are able to. One of the things that is not clear yet is how drowsy the state of consciousness of most people is. We are very much lulled to sleep and dream even in waking consciousness.

The hypnotism in Kali Yuga is very strong. We are all tied in to the matrix very strongly. Also, and maybe especially, people who believe themselves to be very spiritual folks. We socialise with people who are also very much hypnotised and hope that they will help us to wake up. We read many books that strengthen our hypnosis. We do programs in personal development and spirituality that oftentimes again deepen our ignorance and suffering.

We keep on giving power to our mind instead of practising devotion to Shiva or the Great Goddess. The way to Shiva (pure and undifferentiated consciousness) is through Shakti (the world process). The Great Goddess is the entire world process. We have to experience the entire world process. The world process is not to be shunned. It is to be embraced, as it will bring us the salvation and highest experience possible.

Remember that Lord Shiva was already a total renunciate while meditating in the forest and in the ice. Then Shakti (in the form of Parvati) drew him out into the world. That is how he came to the highest possible realisation. Through his wife! The highest realisation is total and complete. It did not come about by practising celibacy, but through lovemaking. We have to make love with the entire world. Shake and let go.

This is especially true in Vamachari as one of the hidden meanings of 'vama' is beauty. In the left-handed Vamachari we very much emphasise and incorporate beauty. Many schools are very austere and practitioners have to deprive their mind of input, they have to starve the senses, and torture the body, or they are brainwashed by horrible concepts like sin and guilt with which it is totally impossible for anyone to ever be happy. They allow themselves to be very much restricted. And these poor people are willing to defend their 'fate' with their life, so deeply does it go. They are not at all sure about the God that they worship. They cannot point to Him and have never even seen Him ...
It might be good for you to contemplate what you are very sure of.

Of the thing that you know, what do you believe to be true and what do you really know to be true or real for sure. From this distinction you start to practise philosophy. With precision. When you can go no further it is up to you whether you want to embrace theology, but don't go into all sorts of silly ideas and mind-traps. Don't be fluffy, but very precise.

We see the God that we worship everywhere. Especially in the suffering and the poor. Being with these people and trying to help them is the highest worship.

But we also have rituals with lots of beauty. Beauty in 900 AD was slightly different than in 2002. We use all our senses to become aware of beauty and to become deeply impregnated with beauty. So deeply that the beauty seduces us inwards. We do not speed up the mind into a hyper-state of euphoria, but we still the mind into a deep state of bliss. It is the great exponent of Advaita – Sri Adi Shankar himself – who wrote the famous tantriç text Saundaryalahari. It means the wave of beauty. With great detail he describes the beautiful and young Goddess Tripura from her head down to her toes. There is also another text called the wave of bliss. In his external life – because of all the vigorous debating, especially with Buddhists – he propagated Advaita, but in his heart and soul he was most likely a tantrik. Adi Shankar founded four monasteries to uphold the light of the non-dual wisdom.

They are ashrams headed by a Shankaracharya. I wrote about His Divinity Swami Brahmamanda Sarasvati Jagadguru Bhagwan Shankaracharya of Jyotir Mat. In these ashrams they practise Shakti-worship. This means they worship the Divine Mother. One of his disciples – the now famous Maharishi Mahesh Yogi from the TM-movement – also worships (or worshipped; that I do not know) a rubi yantra and thereby one of the manifestations of the Divine Mother, most likely Tripura Sundari.

This worship is always surrounded by lots of beauty. They try to make the beauty as intense and beautiful as possible. These people always live a simple life and virtually all the resources available are channelled into increasing the beauty of the worship. That is why I emphasise that you should dress most beautifully in tantric gatherings. Shower. Wear fresh clothes. Put on nice perfume (maybe sandalwood). Have sweet breath (tantriks often put a clove underneath their tongue). Use candles, incense and lights

Vaidyanatha Varakale was born in 1903 in a special family in India. At the age of 16 he was initiated in Sri Vidya and worshipped the goddess Tripura. As a result of very strong devotion (Shaktipata) and faithful practice he received a vision of the sage Durvasas. He taught him the exact method of Sambhava Yoga out of the Trika system. This is a vast and highly refined system for the total enfoldment of our full spiritual potential. He practised this Sambhava method and as a result realised the main principles of what he only later found out to be Kashmir Saivism.

He later became famous under the name Amrtavagbhava. He wrote many philosophical texts, mostly hymns to Lord Shiva. At the age of 25 he started to wander through the Himalayas. Beautiful visions kept coming and he kept on producing beautiful poetry and philosophical discourses.

He was astonished to find in the works of Abhinavagupta, Somamanda and Utpaladeva exactly the same philosophical principles that were revealed to him at a young age by Durvasas in 'a dream'. This is the difference that I tried to describe between a scholar and a practitioner (tantrik, devotee, disciple). Remember the story of the great Swami Muktananda. Of everything that was available, he also found that Kashmir Saivism best described his yogic experiences.

Acarya Amrtavagbhava wrote strongly about what he called 'Vilasa'. This is the blissful and stirring sexual interaction with a lover who is both virile and at ease due to complete freedom and transcendence of time. It is a sort of playful, radiant, spontaneous and leisurely form of erotic play. It describes the amorous couple during the most enticing and rapture-filled exchange. 'Las' is dance and beauty. According to Kashmir Saivism, the whole universe, all phenomena and all functions are the manifestation of the divine exuberance (vilasa) of the non-dualistic Absolute.

We are aiming at self-knowledge. But by self-knowledge we do not mean understanding the personality. You'll have to transcend. Abide in the Self. Discover where 'the push' and 'the pull' in yourself come from. Renounce the renunciation. Embrace. Tantra is a loving embrace.

Many people make all sorts of horizontal movements while I am talking about a huge vertical move. A great and deep dive. A plunge into the Unknown. I explained how science is the opposite of mysticism. Many people are interested in exploring mysticism, but insist on holding on to the ideas that they have gathered. Of what use is that? Mention to me one worthwhile idea. I already hear X say "The importance of loving one another". Yeah, but the one person you love today, you want to slaughter tomorrow when you find out that he loves another as well. Is that the love you so much want to protect?

No my friends. It is obvious that that cannot be real love. It is just very childish. I am looking for people who want to mature. People who strongly feel and sense that there is more than this crazy matrix-stuff. But you need to be vigilantly aware! For me you are never ugly, but what is the resistance to beauty? Didn't Trinity also wear black leather pants?

Spirituality and Afflictions upon Humanity

Don't allow 'spirituality' to become another trap.

There are things that are more holy than your spiritual quest.

Don't ride roughshod over people while you are on the way to your spiritual lecture.

Why would you fight with people over the righteousness of your spiritual idea(l)s?

Try to already be in the spirit while you are on the way to realising your spiritual ideals.

Our only spiritual ideal should be to live in and with the Spirit.

That doesn't mean that you should pride yourself on talking with spirits.

When you would truly live in and with the Spirit, is there any excuse for being impatient? For ridiculing someone? For becoming angry? For defending yourself? For showing off?

Spirituality is not an illusory castle that the ego needs to defend.

Your quest is going well when you leave no traces, but only a beautiful fragrance.

A spiritual lecture may be very important to attend, but it is not necessarily more important than the way.

A spirited debate sometimes happens, but only love really wins.

Some people are proud winning with their mouth, but can you be a conqueror of hearts?

A mind can impress another mind but only a heart can melt.

Only a heart can conquer a heart.

This heart is a no-mind. A no-mind does not conquer.

A no-mind cares and sends out vibrations of love.

It is a wounded and painful heart that feels these vibrations of love.

No mind can cure a wounded heart.

Brilliant minds do superb heart-surgeries.

But these surgeries always leave traces and stitches.

You CAN be a great heart-surgeon. There is not really a school or a training for it other than life.

When you take life it steers you to become a heart-surgeon.

Let life take you.

Forget about spirituality for a while.

Left and right are not that important.

Let people say what they want to say. They will always say something!

But who are you? Who do you know yourself to be regardless of what they say and what you think?

What is your capacity to care about a stranger?

What is your capacity to love someone who is ugly?

What is your capacity to hold someone who does not believe what you believe?

What is your capacity to give away of your possessions?

How deep does your faith run?

What is more important than your capacity to care, to love, to caress, to give away and to have faith?

An idea perhaps?

What do the mind and the ego want to hold on to, despite all that you by now know and experience?

Of course you have duties, children, a job, responsibilities. You have your challenges as I have mine. But what is wisdom?

Your duties and responsibilities are in the mind aren't they? Can you point to them? Do they exist outside of the matrix?

What is your highest responsibility, if there is such a thing?

Do you live in accordance with this 'highest responsibility'?

Are you able to respond?

Do you respond to the call or do you try not to hear it?

How sincere is your spiritual quest? What non-spiritual sacrifices did you make in order to make so-called spiritual progress?

How is spirituality different from your capacity to care, to love, to caress, to give (away) and to have faith?

Is a highly evolved spiritual person any other than a real human being?

Who or what is that real human being?

Then what are the five billions people who walk, talk, sit, gesture, eat and drink from, excrete on and lie on the globe?

Are our walks, talks, gestures, eating, drinking and excretions all lies?

Are our perceptions a lie?

Do we dream in a dream?

How can we know for sure?

You may say that you feel that there is more to life than this.

You've experienced glimpses of a real, deep and profound love.

Why is this love hidden?

Or are we simply blind?

What will restore our sight?

By which miracle will we start to really hear?

Do you feel very strong or do you feel hopeless?

Are you very clear or are you more and more confused?

Do you somewhere sense that feeling very strong and being very clear is better than feeling hopeless and being confused?

Who is the one who senses that?

What else does this 'one' sense, know, think, feel and hold on to?

What if you let it all go?

Where would that leave you?

A hint from the dark....

Peace & Violence

We should never forget that in the eye of the hurricane there is perfect stillness.

In the animal kingdom there is always fighting and violence.

Mother earth always has volcanic eruptions and floods.

The delivery of a child is painful. Death however can be very peaceful.

Life forces itself in these ways.

Who is to say that men should not fight battles? Maybe it is life itself that pushes itself this way.

Isn't it the case that most people who want peace are violent themselves? In every house there is violence.

There is no attainment of peace without violence. There is no violence without peace. All these opposites are there, and they most likely are there to teach us the possibility of transcending. We have to become a witness.

Maybe all the people who are very much engaged in prayer should resort to more violence. What have they all suppressed? Who knows what gets amplified and fortified by their religious prayers and rituals? Did they have the effect that they said? So much about these practices...

And who knows what it will bring? We are not to judge. There is thesis and anti-thesis. Striving towards peace will create violence. Any mind is violent. That is the nature of the mind. The mind is the one who does not accept and fights. 'Peace of mind' does not exist at all. A mind is never in peace. It is always on the move. All of existence is moving. The entire galaxy is moving. The big question is what is it moving towards? And we already know that it is moving towards its own extinction.

Consciousness is moving. Through the veils it created the mind and the body. Both are characterised by movement. What are the movements of the body? Eating, walking, talking. Even while we walk we are never in the moment. We are always talking. Or we are going somewhere. We are worried. Or we are in a hurry. Why the hurry? Because we are engrossed and trapped by 'time'. We identify with the body and this identification creates a sense of urgency.

The identification leads to preservation. We want to live long, which is a fallacy. We have nothing to do with the body. It is not the mind or the ego that is moving the body. That is a false thought. It is existence itself that is moving. It is consciousness itself that is pro-creating. We are merely a witness.

The body sleeps, lies, sits, excretes, eats, drinks and works. You have nothing to do with it. All these things are happening. You do not have to worry about money. The money that you need will come.

It is the mind that always worries. Who wants to have more? It is not enough or not good enough. These are all the tricks of the mind. The mind wants to possess, but what it says or thinks that it possesses, it never really possesses. Life shows that. You think you possess a lot of money and it is gone. You think you have health and the health disappears. You think you own your husband and another woman takes his body. You think you own your children and they are gone, doing things you would never approve of. You have self-esteem and even that gets smashed. You are happy and the next day you are in despair.

The wise say that there is only one way to be steady, and that is by acquiring the steady state. This requires soul over mind. But we have to work in order to progress towards a steady state. It does not come about by itself. There seems to be something that a human being can do. Amidst of all the tragedies and violence of life, we can work to acquire a steady state. Not based on any suppression! Merely on wisdom. The wisdom of disidentification. 'I am not the body'. 'I am not the mind'.

Through this disidentification, a deeper love comes. This love is not bodily based. Now we feel the love when there is a body. Without the body it is difficult to love. One month after the death of the body of the beloved, we still love the idea of the person. A year later the love has changed. There is more acceptance. This is mental love. After five years the mourning is over. There is acceptance and a faint, heavenly love. Love grows in gratitude. The highest love that we can experience is spiritual love.

The devotion is towards a certain energy. We could call it God. When the devotion matures, it becomes Self-referral. This is the meaning of the word 'Namah' as in 'Om Namah Shivaya'. We recognise this energy in ourselves and finally we recognise that we are that energy and have been that energy all along. There is nothing else but this energy. It is in us and all around us. Nothing is separated from that energy.

This energy that we recognise, we are and have been all along, and then we see and experience that all around us is nothing other than consciousness. It is the Shakti of Shiva. The moving-consciousness is the mirror reflection of silent and pure awareness. It is moving. It is vibrating. It moves us and the entire galaxy. We are at the centre. We have moved to the axis. Even time and space revolve around us, but we are not affected by time and space. Time and space come and go but we are always there. The body may die and decay, but that has no effect on this awareness that we are. The body is merely a dress of this awareness. Just like a body puts on a dress, wears it and takes it off, so this awareness takes on many forms. It enjoys these forms (e.g. through the nervous system) and disposes of them. The awareness (Shiva) remains unaffected.

Just as we like to wear all kinds of clothes, this awareness also likes all sorts of dresses and forms. Just as sometimes we are sleepy, sometimes we feel romantic and sometimes we are angry and we want to destroy, so it is for Existence. Sometimes Life is very romantic. It seduces and makes love. Consciousness pro-creates. It finds nourishment. It is naughty. It betrays others. It surely betrays the mind. That is why we and Hafiz talk about the greatest Magician. Life teases and life destroys. This Life is also seemingly cruel. But only from the perspective of the mind. Awareness is merely playful and that is it! Also the violence and the terrorism is a show of its playfulness and incredible diversity. In the playfulness some have more and some have less. But this is only seemingly so. We all have access to the same wealth.

And let it be very clear that more poor people have access to this (discovered) internal wealth than the rich. The rich are guarding their 'riches'. The poor do not have to guard their riches. They just share their wealth. So what are you so busy for? Why don't you wake up and come and sit next to me? Why don't you relax a bit more and enjoy? Why all the hurry and worry? We should never forget that in the eye of the hurricane there is perfect stillness.

This life has only one producer. Many new age people like to believe that they are the producer and they are very busy visualising and wishing. All this wishing is also a sort of violence.

Every wish is based on non-acceptance. It is now important to make major progress in non-dualism. A mind has nothing to do with realisation or enlightenment. Really try to pierce what it is. And after that still try to understand why we act and create beauty. But first come to fully understand the word 'yoga'. It comes before 'beauty'. Yoga you see is not something that you do, 'perform' or practise. Yoga happens. It is indeed true that the rishis gave out certain exercises (postures). But the point was about awareness. Later on the impostors said that it would bring longevity and 'peace of mind'. You have to use your buddhi (higher mind, self or pure intellect). Otherwise you will be deceived as so many people are.

And now people are enticed to do something that they hope will bring them peace of mind, or that will make them look more beautiful or live longer. All these are not the original teachings. This is the rape in the 21st century. There is only ONE illness and only ONE wealth! For that cure and discovery, service, surrender and the willingness to sacrifice, are not unimportant. All along I have spoken about the importance of self-inquiry. Kashmir Saivism is the doctrine of Grace. That is it. All is Grace. We can work with and on refinement and even that – I explained thoroughly – is the operation of Grace. In order to make any sincere spiritual progress, we need to be touched by Grace.

That is why 'touch' is something very beautiful in the Path of Yoga, Beauty & Delight. But it is not (only) the human touch. I am really talking about the divine touch. When we have that infusion of Spirit, the path of true and authentic spirituality starts. And that is not attaching one mind-idea on to another. It is not talking about a no-mind state with our mind. We cannot and will not know the Unknown through the known. There are thousands of people who can do that and you must learn to differentiate. Be very careful of which teacher you are with. There are so many impostors. And all these impostors have a certain task. They are all Shiva. All have their place in the play of consciousness. All is designed for us to come to awareness.

An impostor however will not be able to take away the veils. Use your intellect. Only with the higher intellect (buddhi) can we come to know the cunning ways of the mind. And by recognising all the cunning and deceitful ways of the mind, we can come to know our soul and rest in our heart. If you are very smart, you can come to see the veils, even with an impostor. Only Grace lifts the veils. That will be a glorious day for you. In this tradition (YB&D) we do not celebrate our day of birth. We celebrate the day of resurrection. We celebrate the death of the mind. We celebrate our second birth!

It is my most sincere wish – and please don't get me wrong when I use this word 'wish' – to celebrate many of these days of second birth with many of you and much more for many glorious years to come. Rejoice in your own awakening and in the awakening of other people. Therefore you first have to recognise. Follow the Shakti-energy. But most of people follow the stories and the events in life. Follow the patternless pattern back to the source, which is Shiva (awareness).

The refinement is through your mind and senses. You refine your knowing and doing and understand that it is not 'you' who is doing that. It is Grace in operation and you can only be grateful. This gratitude is Love. It is the love that is necessary to stitch.

A no-mind has no judgements. All is fine for him or her. A no-mind has no judgements about lovemaking. Lovemaking is a very important form of doing (kriya) of this consciousness that we are. But you should strive to become a bit more steady. Find the steady-state amidst all the violence and terrorism. And do not fight or object to the terrorism. There is terrorism in every house. There is terrorism in every heart that is not governed by a no-mind (a heart governed by a mind we call 'a shadow'). All the mediocre people write each other mails wishing everyone else love, peace and wisdom. But the hand of a mind that writes 'love' writes 'war' as easily. History and the present prove that over and over again.

Don't be influenced by this sort of hand. Come to know the hand that makes all these hands move. Only that hand holds the master key to liberation. Liberation from mental slavery. There will always be peace and violence. This peace and that violence are part of the noise. Drop the labels and interpretations. Become a Witness of life and watch it all happening. It is the enfoldment of Lord Shiva. Praise him. Move out of the realm of the matrix.

Why has it not happened? First you need to learn about acceptance. You have to learn deep surrender, which is nothing other than the combination of Acceptance and Gratitude. This leads to the devotion that will free you.

The master creates friction in you. He does that on purpose. Together you and him work out tamas-guna in your energy field. Tamas-guna is the inertia, dullness, sleepiness and dark tendencies. You need the heat.

The body is made of earth. That is logical. You eat and drink the products of the earth. Your body is earth. The mind is air. It moves as air. Can't get a grip on it. Consciousness surprisingly is water. Water expresses in the seminal fluid when you are a man. This is the sacredness of creation. The key to life. The great mystery. Maithuna is also a great mystery. When water is heated (lovemaking) it becomes gas. This gas becomes air. This air becomes ether and the ether finally becomes awareness. This is the home-journey. This is all part of the tantric alchemy.

Be sincere in your practice. Watch your thoughts! Disidentify from the movements of your body. That is what we do in tantric rituals. It is about awareness. To not identify. How to go beyond the mental love to a spiritual love. For that we need some heat.

It is much more difficult to heat matter. Water vaporises fairly easily. But how to go beyond the body? To feel, know and realise that the body does not exist? That we do not exist as a separate individual? That there is no birth and no death? That consciousness is the only ever-unchanging reality of Life? And that this consciousness is moving? This is quite a process requiring refinement, awareness and heat. I first work with people in expanding their sense of multi-dimensional awareness. And this surprisingly goes together with the love and devotion. The more love and devotion, the more growth in multi-dimensional awareness. It is not a process of the mind. The mind is preventing. It wants to hold on to the known. The mind wants a certain spiritual technique so that it can hold on to something and affirm a tight grip. That is just spiritual conditioning.

Tantra is freedom, and understand very well that it is the shared responsibility of your master and you to work out the tamas guna in you. All is the play of consciousness. There is and will be violence. A birth is violent. Animals fight. That is their nature. It is the nature of a mother chicken sometimes – after they have hatched – to destroy her children. Eagles are thrown out of the nest.

Why don't you ease up? Why waste so much energy?

Life is forcing itself on us. You believe that you act but it is simply life expressing itself in a myriad ways. You want to unravel the matrix? Become a weaver. Tantra is weaving. You can learn to follow the Shakti-energy.

When someone throws me a stone it is my choice whether I catch it, look at it, throw it back, duck, hold up a mirror, get hurt or transform the stone into a jewel. There is evolution amidst revolution and revolution amidst evolution. I like both!

There is harmony amidst diversity and diversity is part of harmony. How can we speak of harmony when there is no diversity? So rejoice in the diversity and try to become aware of and to see the underlying unity as part of multi-dimensional awareness. Most important is, of course, that which I have least spoken and lectured about, namely Essence. Essence is non-dualistic in nature. Nobody can speak about 'it' or explain 'it'. We can only point or hint. We can say what it is not, but we can only experience 'it' in our awareness. And only when we shed the entire mind and all it's programming, tendencies and conditioning.

Animal Liberation Day

Today – October 4 – is World Liberation Day for animals.

A young guy had been reading about Tantra at school and when he got home he told his father that he had learned that in the old days they performed animal sacrifices. He asked his father whether they still do these things these days. The father answered: Yes my son they still do, except now the preacher says – in front of the sacrificial altar – "I hereby proclaim you husband and wife!".

Animal sacrifice is a good custom. It is a shame that people don't do it anymore these days. It is such a profound ritual to take the animal and to slaughter it on the altar. They did it a lot with sheep.

These days animals are treated like pigs. At the most holy celebrations folk eat dead turkey. There is no more bond with nature. No awareness that the food, which we eat, is in fact ourselves. Hardly any respect. We are very much cut off from nature. Man has become the most dangerous animal roaming around on this planet. No other animal is safe from him. We eat other animals but don't even realise that the meat was an animal. In the far past men hunted the animals together and they grew to respect the animals.

Some ancient civilisations performed an animal sacrifice, which was a symbol for the sacrifice of their inner animal. It is that animal that needs to be slaughtered. The lower self or the animal must be sacrificed to the higher self. This animal that is nothing else but greed, lust, hate, shame, jealousy, anger, conditional love, selfishness and control.

We do not want to be a primitive civilisation, but we are. There is no control over our stomach and our mouth. Our mouth should be connected with our heart but it is not. It is merely an extension of the stomach. We throw it full of stuff, and of course 'stuff ' comes out. In Tantra the mouth is considered to be even more 'dirty' than our anus. Imagine the harm that people commit with their mouths ...

These primitive people had better take a long period of silence to learn something valuable in life. They like to get their teeth into meat, but that meat is contaminated. They enjoy rotting flesh. And are very proud of it. When they go on vacation, one of the most important things is the taste of the meat that they put their teeth into. And today these hypocrites celebrate Animal Liberation day...

I think we should re-install the custom of animal sacrifice!

The world is becoming a dangerous place with all these sheep bleating around. Man has to excel himself. We have to grow into something higher than we currently are. For that we need to become fearless. We have to be willing to sacrifice our lower nature. That is what Tantra is about. We unleash the tiger within. It eats up the sheep of the unconscious mind, which is merely an automaton. A sheep is a slave. A sheep does as directed. Man is not very different. Man thinks himself to be powerful, but is more a slave. A slave of desires and tendencies.

We should learn to refine our senses so that we can pierce the matrix and smell its rotten perfume. We cannot continue being slaves of the media, religion and our parents. The world is in great need of some wise ones. A wise one is he who sacrificed the animal. Don't you remember from some ancient movies that the huge treasure in the jungle was protected on the outside by monkeys and at the core by snakes? The mind is the monkey. We have to learn to silence the monkey. The monkeys are always silenced when the cobra turns up.

Kundalini can only rise when the mind is silenced. When kundalini rises, the monkeys stand aside and merely watch in awe. They know the incredible powers of the snake. Your greatest treasure is protected in the same way. The monkeys (mind) try hard to distract you. That is their job. Your job is to develop heroism. You must defeat the shadow. Give room to the animal within. Get to know him or her. This animal has a strategy and you need to understand this strategy and become even smarter. This is not an easy task.

At any moment the wolf wants to devour the lamb and you must learn what balance and what responsibility is. This is not an intellectual understanding. You must feel it in your body. You have to balance certain energies.

Only then will the snake start her enchanting and hypnotising dance. You will see in paintings and drawings that many of the eastern Gods or God-men are protected by snakes. The snakes arise over their heads. That snake symbolises Ma Kundalini. When Ma Kundalini has risen, she is firm over our head. That man in meditation has learned to tame a tiger. That man immersed in silence sacrificed the animal. His sacrifice was very peaceful. His sacrifice left no traces. Not one drop of blood was spilled.

Animal Liberation is a great thing. But real human liberation is the only liberation for animals. Every animal needs to protect himself against the greatest predator. But, one day nature will rule again. Now man lives in the fantasy that he rules the planet. But nature will make very clear to him how false that is. It will be a very painful day. All his illusions will be shattered. It unfortunately will require a lot of bloodshed. The solution that the rishis and the saints offer is truly peaceful, but it will be ignored. The animal in man is so thirsty for blood, the need for sensation is so high, and he is in fact so primitive that the bloodshed is bound to happen. Mirdad already forecasted ...

So my friends, be wise: liberate the animal within. Set him free. Then become a hunter and hunt her down. And then slaughter the animal. Use the intelligence of Buddhi to sacrifice the lower nature. Do not indulge and do not suppress. Don't let the animal rule you. Look her in the eyes! Get the message of love. Set her free. While you go on the hunt for the animal, you will notice that Life is hunting you. One day you will become so tired that you will fall and submit. That glorious day the Grace will rain upon your heart.

Your heart will blossom and bloom because of the holy Understanding. This we call a lion's heart. This, my dear brothers and sisters, is what we call a disciple.

The Master-polisher and her Assistants

We all know that there is one Master-polisher. The Master-polisher is God. In this philosophy we call her Shakti. Shakti is consciousness. It is purely vibrating consciousness. For jiva, Shakti is the world and the entire world-process. The world and the world-process (maya or matrix) is polishing us all.

The questions that I would like to explore are: what our relationship with this Master-polisher is (who are we when the polishing is finished?) And what the function of a guru or a master is in regard to the Master-polisher.

It would be best if you first do your own contemplations on this subject.

We could say that humans are rocks, and are polished on the way towards becoming diamonds. How does a diamond arise? I don't know all the details, but I guess it has to do with pressure. Do you also feel the pressure of life? Accept it and allow Life to mould you into a diamond. Life itself is the Master-polisher. We call her Shakti. That is why in this non-dual Tantra philosophy we have great reverence for the Goddess.

A rock in a river becomes very smooth over many centuries because of the continuous stream of water that polishes it. In the same way, you are being polished over hundreds of lifetimes by the same stream of water. You can either accept it or resist it. In the end it doesn't matter that much. The stream doesn't care too much about the ideas of the rock. Whatever the rock thinks, it gets polished anyway. Resistance of the individual is part of the polishing process. No one can beat the Master-polisher.

But how is it when the polishing is completed? When the rock has turned into a diamond? It is likely that you will then be totally aligned with the Master-polisher. Many spiritual philosophies talk in this regard about being a servant/instrument of God. No need to assume too much about this; we'll have to find out for ourselves.

But now about the 'role' of a guru or a master. The master is sort of 'an assistant' of the Master-polisher. The Master-polisher is unseen while the master is our living guide. Upon completion we will come vis-à-vis with the Master-polisher. She will not remain hidden anymore.
The living guide sends you back to the unseen guide (the Supreme Being). The unseen guide – the full and glorious realisation of Paramashiva – is your destiny. The living guide (the master) helps to bring you to that destination. He may do that in a revolutionary (unpredictable) way.

Realisation of Paramashiva is the ultimate Truth. The master can only hand you the relative truth. The Truth cannot be spoken about.

So we should try to understand that a fully realised master is sort of the assistant of the unseen guide or the Master-polisher, even though they may work in seemingly different or even opposing ways. There is thesis and anti-thesis.

We are all being polished by the Master-polisher – all the time. Some people also seek the guidance of a living guide. Make sure you understand that process very well. Most people in the spiritual arena are trapped in huge semi-spiritual trips. Devotion is very important. It will support the work of the unseen as well as the living guide. Also exact understanding will be very beneficial for the entire process.

Many people grossly lack the necessary understanding and thus continue in darkness.

It is very natural that when people are serious about awakening, they seek the best living guide that they can find. The key is to anchor yourself with that master so that you can receive all of his or her blessings. Most people keep on shopping around. They are quickly disappointed in their living guide and move on to another, and another, and another... Surely there are lots of gurus in the market place. When you have found a guru where you have strong recognition, you can check and test this person. But always understand that the guru is not the person but it is a principle. A principle that operates through a body that you tend to call the guru.

There is however no denial that some masters are more of a master than others. It depends on how much of their subtle impressions are totally burnt, their level of consciousness and also the tradition that they are trained or initiated in. Some people seem to have more potential than others. When you are with a great master, it is not very useful to still be impregnated by people who are by no means masters, like some slick authors, guru-wannabes and impostors.

A master can come in Indian clothes and in western. He may live a strict celibate life or not. She may speak English with an Indian accent or Swedish. He may be very friendly and it is also possible that he is often angry. I know masters who have many reasons to be frustrated and you can contemplate whether it is possible for an enlightened master to be frustrated. Some masters speak a lot and others are more silent. Some do therapy with students and others do not. Some do rituals and others denounce rituals. Some advise you to study the scriptures and others warn you against the scriptures. Some wear only white clothes and others wear jeans. Some priests set their people up to kill others, but they are surely not masters. One thing I know for sure and that is that a master is not fundamentalist. Some masters like ceremonies and others just roam around freely. Some masters never dance and others like to dance and sing.

It only becomes clear that all these things are not criteria for a mind to judge who is a master and who is not. We can say that a master should have no sexual or power-issues but who is to judge (with which projections?)? It is also not their charisma. It is not their age (Adi Shankar died at the age of 29 and JC at the age of 33 while Mirdad was already a great prophet at the age of 18). It is also not their number of students and disciples

So which criterion to use? The answer is that when the student is ready, the teacher will come. Few people are ready yet. The matrix-life offers great powers of attraction and delusion.

Questions and Contemplations on 'Desiring'

Human beings have many desires.

The irony is that by chasing all their desires, they usually do not get what they are looking for and end up with tremendous suffering.

We are all driven by our desires. We know that we have an ugly beast inside because not all of our desires are fulfilled. We crave for more money, great sex, more vitality, power or we have 'spiritual' desires like an ashram or peace-of-mind. All are leading us to frustration and we don't know what to do with this beast ...

Know your desires. Is it OK for you that we separate desires into those coming from the mind and those from the heart? We will deal with the desires coming from (y)our genitals later on.

We all know what I mean by desires from the mind. They are consumptive. They arise because you see other people having it. They are influenced by advertising. It was not on your shopping list, but you see it in the window and want it. They are based on scarcity and greed. People make € 10.000. Then they move on to € 100.000. That is already quite a sum of money isn't it? Some 'lucky ones' even make a million. But that is, of course, not enough and they continue with bigger projects. For their mind there is no end. Some wing their way to € 10.000.000. Can you believe it that some people even move on to owning a hundred million euros or dollars?

We can all logically conclude that that is enough, but not for these minds. They want a billion and several billions etc. There comes no end. And many of them still feel uncertain, fearful and unfulfilled. The wisdom has not come in their poor minds!

What are desires of the heart?

There are people who say that whatever men look for, in everything that they are chasing after and pursuing, ultimately they are all looking for one thing. All the people on the planet long for the same thing but go about it in different ways. What is this one craving or yearning? What is the longing of every person?

Why don't you look inside and try to answer this question. The homework is to understand that desires are not bad. The fulfilment of one desire leads to another desire. Are you, however, going horizontally or vertically? We do not have to suppress our desires, but some profound understanding would be nice. Start to understand that there are desires from the genitals, the mind (what is the difference...?) and the heart.

But what do we do with our ego-desires? Pray for some evolution to happen? Focus on niscam seva and suppressing them? Or do we do self-inquiry and dismantle the 'desirer'? Will everybody then become poor? Will we all give our riches away?

What is beautiful about desires?

Didn't God also have a sort of desire?

Maybe she is desiring through us?

What does that require of us?

What does Zorba-the-Buddha mean in this regard?

What is your solution for desires of the genitals?

What is in fact the problem with indulging?

Where and who would you be without desires?

A person who desires to have no desires typifies the trap in spirituality.

Spiritual philosophies disagree – as you know – in how to deal with desires. That starts in their understanding of what a desire is. Some people see a desire as an implant from the devil. A mind always looks at desires through the polarity of 'good & bad'.

What does desire have to do with fear? I heard president Bush say: "We refuse to live in fear!" and that apparently justifies his attack on Iraq.

Some people adopt a philosophy that everything is fine and perfect, that there is nothing to do or to improve upon, that they are not the doer and that there is no such thing as responsibility. Would you like to have such a happy person as your neighbour? Can you imagine how an entire village with these kind of people would be?

Michelangelo was very inspired (in spirited) and it is very natural that this inspiration likes to see itself expressed in the form. Upon completion all form may disappear again and only the most concentrated 'form' of beauty and bliss remains. You do not need to wait that long however. You are also in-spirited. The great spirit lives in you. It beckons you to sublimate without rejection. How can you answer that call?

Emotional Deficiency and Love

Today let's take a HOT topic.

HOT for almost everyone involved.

I will, however, write this presuming you have a partner, like you are married or living together. Excuse me for the bourgeois presupposition that it is one guy with one gall ...

It comes as no surprise to anyone – probably – that it seems like these days building a relationship is even more challenging than ever before. This is probably because of the stars, Kali Yuga and the current energy influenced by demographics and rapid changes in social structures.

There are plenty of ways for love. How about the following:

" When I think of * it is like 1000 litres of snow melting in my head and then it suddenly begins to boil."

The love between a totally realised soul and a disciple or friend, is the easiest and most expansive that exists. Well, lets say very expansive because any relationship built on the right fundament can take you all the way. But it is not easy. It requires each person to have Holy Insight, or in simple terms, proper understanding. That we are here not to claim each other, but to inspire each other in love and wisdom.

But this is easier said then done. Why? Because we are not free. We are caught. Most people are still in the grip of the patterns and nets of their parents. One child is sexually molested and when he grows up he does the same. And his children, and so on. NOW is a very precious opportunity for billions of people on the planet to change that pattern. How? By aligning to the ONE patternless pattern.

Let's begin to understand and admit that our parents were emotionally deficient. We were not brought up with the love and warmth that we needed and desired. That does not imply that our entire life will be a defect. We can heal. How? We need to be showered with love and this will never happen when we demand it. We can only give it. In the Order of the Holy Fire the strongest shower of love attainable is the holy fire.

Make sure you never turn into a bookkeeper because then all will be lost.

Your partner needs lots of warmth and love from you. More than you ever received. And it is part of the magical universe that you can! Yes! You can. You have it. You lack nothing once you start to focus on giving, you will realise that you are sitting on an eternal fountain of love and it never runs dry. This is why we practise devotion and surrender.

Our movement will be wet, hot and juicy. I don't like this dry stuff of so many other organisations. Young and old people all can be juicy. ALIVE! God is not boring.
No matter how your partner treats you 'bad', you can (be the wise one and) continue to give love and to work to warm that person out of the ice (isolation; ice-nation). The ice-nation is the matrix. We are creating the Magical Carpet by spreading, weaving and blending. These are the magical words.

In our relationship we must be willing to sacrifice. We should let go of how we think it should be or what you deserve. You are getting what you deserve. This has to do with past impressions and patterns. Allow the wisdom of Tantra (and the masters) to guide you. If you are lucky, some of these patterns will be burnt and you will be set a bit more free. This usually however takes many more lifetimes to complete. You focus on this life by weaving, making sure you leave no trace behind. Be willing to accept a life of great sacrifice, suffering and surrender. Your happiness will come in the surrender. They are the same. Surrender really means letting go. It is an active form of love whereby you let go of everything and are receptive. Surrender implies gratitude and wisdom.

Fine Tuning

Dear readers!

Many of you have heard the difference between reading a text and drinking a text, yet very few know the difference.

This book can be a goldmine, but you could totally miss the point. In fact several readers do! Kashmir Saivism and YB&D is a philosophy, but differently from how people understand this word. We should maybe say that it is a no-mind philosophy.

I had the good fortune to be with very intelligent and highly interesting people. Some C.E.O.'s, wealthy people, some gypsies, some unemployed, several very attractive women, some lunatics, weirdoes, some people with a high IQ. Many people with a bad sense of humour, and a few blessed souls who understand my humour, but that is very and – in fact – exceptionally rare.

Some people have read a lot, have been to all kinds of personal development and especially semi-spiritual seminars and they know a lot. But what is the use of all this lot that you know? Many of these people could be busy like this for several more lifetimes. And thus you are entirely missing the point of these texts. In fact it is an insult to me if you are with us like this.

But why would you need many?

Why would you take only one?

Both can be a fear. Both can be a commercial trick. What is the difference between guidance and misguidance? Maybe we do not need an external teacher and have to discover our inner master? In Tantra we have to be – usually for several lifetimes – with a master. How else will we get our nectar? Try to understand how you are influenced by the current circumstances, conditioning and chain-of-events.

Reading 100 more spiritual bestsellers and going to another 10 retreats and supposedly great masters might not do the trick for you.

Mysticism goes beyond the question of guidance and misguidance as long as we understand the difference between white and black magic. Mysticism is a system that has been designed to ultimately 'force' you out of the mind and into the heart. Mysticism such as Tantra can never be understood by the mind in one lifetime. A mind has absolutely no grip on mysticism. That is why not many people are interested in it. It is simply too vast and too complicated. So only one road remains open and that is the road that is displayed in front of you.

I have the good fortune to be with a couple of people who set out to discover the joy of devotion. What happens for them just cannot be described in words. They are now engaged in a cosmic, universal and in fact inter-galactic love affair, which they didn't know existed, even though several have been with great masters. And that is the only way to receive the Gifts in Tantra.

It is important to understand here that the teaching does not primarily go through words. We use words all right. For you, reading these words well is very important. While we use words, the sword is also going around and those who are most ready benefit. But there is something else which might be even more valuable. That, which leads into the no-mind experience; that which we call drinking. You can listen to 100 gurus but when none of them teaches you how to drink, not much is happening. In fact you are being misled when there is no nectar or Living Water.

A great master can be silent for a year. And even though he says nothing, people can learn more than by following all the great and popular weekend workshops in Amsterdam or L.A for a year.

When we say that the Path of Yoga, Beauty & Delight is a Path of the Heart, we also mean that the important teachings go via the heart, and not the mind. Only very few people have discovered this. The guru-sisya parampara is 'powered' by devotion. Otherwise the blending in alchemy is impossible to achieve and dangerous to perform.

JC was very lucky with Mary.

And you will be very lucky if you learn to drink. In order to learn to drink, you need an inner – very aware, grateful, alert and receptive – attitude and a devotional heart. This devotional heart is the toughest for most. You want to accomplish it all via the mind or choose to shut the mind off and dwell in a sort of nihilistic state towards which there are multiple warnings in non-dualistic Kashmir Saivism. If we do not involve the heart, most of our efforts will be in vain.

So if you keep reading with your mind only, you are missing the point. So what to do? I hope that I gave the answer.

If you didn't dig it try the following: Imagine that you live many centuries ago and that you have several questions about life that are hard to answer. Then this unknown wildman sends you a scroll every now and then for free. They seem to contain an incredible wisdom. But only when you treat them as the most important gift in your life and read them with all attention and with candlelight will the honey turn into nectar.

Divine Madness, Non-doership and Double Absence

We have talked extensively about Divine Madness, but no talking about it will bring it to us. And we will not be able to find 'it' as no mind will ever be able to even fathom what Divine Madness is or looks like.

I can tell you what it is. Divine Madness is the same as non-doership.

Divine Madness has nothing to do with the mind or any structure in the matrix that the mind upholds.

And yet our ship is setting course to this I-land. It must be that this is a magical ship then. That's right, the Ishvara-ship.

But are you sure you want to board? There are many other ships. Many have much more luxury. More security. Others promise you 'happiness' or that you will find 'the love of your life'. Again others tell you that you can learn with them how to fulfil your dreams and desires.

Here there is none of that. 'Remember, all that I am offering is the Truth!'

So we have to start with a very intensive process of disidentifying with the mind and the body. We have to leave all our understanding of the mind behind, no matter how proud we are of its accomplishments. In the mind we have knowledge. But this unfortunately has nothing to do with Understanding or Holy Insight. We may be proud of the knowledge that we have gathered. You may feel that it really helps you. You feel you cannot do without it. It is like

Enzo told Jacques in the diving cabin: 'I was so in love with this girl I thought I couldn't live without her. Two years later I couldn't even remember her name!'

In YB&D you first seek the blessing of Lord Shiva or your master before any important undertaking.
In the West people look up to successful people (the so-called...). In the East the people who are most revered are the masters of wisdom. Even the great politicians and businessmen prostrate before the guru.

How to attain those blessings?

Because the master sees through all sabotage-mechanisms and manipulations, we have to approach him or her very sincerely, really and authentically. We literally offer our head (mind-knowledge).

The blessings are always with us. The entire creation is the enfoldment of Grace. Even when a loved one dies. When there is a cruel war. When you go broke. When you have sincere physical pain and discomfort. When you feel betrayed or are in an argument. Kashmir Saivism welcomes all these moments to come to realisation. Life continuously offers us an opportunity to come to realisation. When you are insulted, only someone who does not know him- or herself can be insulted. How can a wise man be insulted? He knows that he is not the body and not the mind. He is firmly established in consciousness. Nothing in his mind is attached to any idea that could insult him.

Everything that we do is happening. Life is happening and simultaneously the mind identifies and thinks it is the doer. Mind is busy labelling and protecting. No label has any effect on that which is unutterable. And, as Mirdad says, you are the Unutterable uttered forth. Mind tries to protect its position and the only effect is that life is killed. Of course mind can never kill life, but for that temporary and unreal experiencer (mind), Life is not present; only the matrix experience.

And in this matrix-experience we are busy with controlling and structuring. The mind feels it can 'really' control things and structure life. The mind gains incredible false powers. These powers – which are unreal to begin with – further tighten us down into duality and thus suffering. We imagine that we feel the suffering of other people while we are totally unaware of our own enormous suffering. We are tossed around in the extremes of love and hate, beauty and ugliness, good and bad, capable and incapable, success and failure, understanding and confusion etc. Life is continuously moving and at very high speeds. Very high speeds.

The mind is at a much lower speed and the body altogether at an even lower speed. Yet in order to feel the divine pulsation (Spanda) we have to slow down.

Only in the silence will we feel the oscillation of Life. Nobody is able to explain to you the Beyond. The master can take you to the limits of your mind. There he can show you the doorway (because you are on the edge) but you are the one who has to step through it!

That is the field of non-doing. The body may still move, talk, eat and do things. No problem. But you are in the field of not-doing. From there everything starts to make sense. Now the Understanding may happen. From this field the Holy Insight will dawn. This Holy Insight is not expressed in words; it is nectar that you drink. It is none other than ecstasy. This is the delight of Yoga. Yoga I understood to mean YOU GO! So when you as the mind goes (is gone), the real experience of Yoga happens. When the mind is very busy interpreting, everything will be misinterpreted. All the 'misinterpretations' will ultimately guide you to understanding. So all is well. There are no mistakes.

We will find our steadiness but only in the unsteadiness. The mind will never find steadiness in structures, as these structures are not real. They are all part of the illusion. Nothing in the matrix will provide us with what we are looking for. The entire matrix is designed to put you to sleep and to hold you asleep. Why? So that you can wake up and realise (the fifth power of Shiva). But take it easy. All is the operation of Grace. This Grace comes to you as self-efforts.

You reading these words is Grace. Nothing prevents you right now from realising the operation of Grace. Non-dual Kashmir Saivism is merely the description of the operation of Grace. But that is not '*merely*', as it is very full and complete. Matrix is the fourth power of Shiva, namely obscuration. And always fully understand that Shiva in this philosophy is not so much a God or a godly person, but the name that we use to indicate this magical awareness without quality and boundaries. That awareness which is luminous and transcendent. Awareness always aware of itself and thus fully knowing. A human being is affected by this obscuration and thus clouded in partial understanding. When Grace happens, all the clouds of limited knowing, limited creativity and false identification disappear and we shine in our glorious true existence, which is Shiva.

What is left for us then is the watching of (while the body engages in) the enfoldment of Life and we call that play Divine Madness.

Is it now becoming clear to you?

This was written by the hand of Ralph Nataraj, as an operation of Grace. All is the Grace of Lord Shiva. To the double absence I bow (the absence of ourselves still refers to its presence. So when there is absence even to the presence that the absence of ourselves indicates, that is called the double absence).

Appendix

The Tantra academy of five floors.

Tantra means many things to many people. On the website http://www.kundalini.nu you can read the 23 definitions that Ralph wrote in his book Shiva in 2000. It is the most comprehensive, concise and authentic explanation of Tantra that exists. They are a gift and an indication from a master from the Himalayas.

How to practise Tantra in the West? Tantra is love, but it also means order and discipline. Tantra is not hedonism. It carries great depth and requires infinite expansion of consciousness. Tantra very much is a tradition of mastery. It is the mysticism and shamanism from the Himalayas. It has always been an oral tradition.

It is true that your lover can be the one who opens inner doors for you and initiates you into the sacred realm. Yet Tantra is very vast. There are many scriptures and guidelines in Tantra. One can get lost in an endless maze or stuck in a mirage or delusion. We can practise Tantra solitary but the real beauty arises in interaction.

Ralph designed 'the tantric academy' especially for westerners who want to tread the path of Tantra in a modern AND in an authentic way. Open your third eye and share the following vision, which is yours:

Imagine a pyramid. You enter on the first floor and exit at the top. The pyramid may be actual and/or astral. It is permeated with occult powers. It is the most powerful vehicle for tantric transformation (alchemy) and final liberation. It is the very embodiment of Yoga, Beauty & Delight. Everybody is welcome to enter and share the world of magic.

1th.On the first floor people can basically do what they want. The person who is only busy with and interested in the level of the personality, senses and the outer life will not move beyond the first floor. When they are through with it, they can move to the second level.

2nd.The passage to the second floor is an initiation into the mystic Order of the Holy Fire. It sort of requires one to shed the previous religious life and to embrace the mysticism, the technology and the protection of the Masters of the Far East. It also is a pledge towards the Order of the Holy Fire, its sacraments and ones fullest enfoldment.

Entering the second floor means being willing to abandon many of the things one was involved in on the first floor like laziness, inertia, drugs, sex and masturbation. It signifies the practice of great refinement. The '2nd floor' is a thorough training in personal development and is aimed at emotional maturity and steadiness. When this maturity and steadiness has been acquired, you are encouraged to move to level three.

3th.The third floor is spiritual apprenticeship. There is the complete exploration into the mythical domain. There are many secret initiations there. It is also about peaking intellectual development and the study of fine arts.

4th.On the fourth floor we start with the study and practice of tantric alchemy. It is the initiation in the mystery school.

5th.Only a few will be able to reach the fifth floor. The fifth floor is Tantra par excellence including the great rite. This rite allows passage into freedom and liberation from all dogma, inhibitions and ...

The Path of Yoga, Beauty & Delight is unique in that you are advised to first try the highest path (sambahava, the pathless path). Most people need a preparation for the highest teachings and that is what the Order of the Holy Fire is for.

Joining the Order is simple. Your wish is enough. You do not need to pay us, nor is it necessary to change something in your life.

The spiritual path knows several phases and stages. Each stage serves to prepare you for the next. You decide the speed with which you go. The spiritual path is a celestial speed-up. In the Holy Order it is a forcible transformation. This requires you always to prepare for the next initiation and to celebrate life now.

Everybody – or at least the vast majority of the people – enters the Order by the first floor, in which everything is all right and fine. The kundalini-sadhana is only for those who want, have recognition and hear the Calling. To go to the second floor (virtual), it requires you to be initiated and to actively seek the blessings of the wisdom-goddess(es). Also you will receive the guidance of an *elder* on this path and personal instructions for your spiritual practice (kundalini-sadhana). This may require a healthy lifestyle, the practis
ce of a certain mantra and yoga- or breathing exercises. All the while you learn more about the dazzling philosophy of Yoga, Beauty & Delight and there are many stimulating gatherings to attend if you so desire.

When someone is ready for the third floor, the sadhana increases with e.g. the siddhi-techniques for inner perfection. Over a period of a year you learn sutras for every chakra. You learn to balance energies which are difficult to bear. There are many programs for people on the third floor like Gurdjieff temple-dances, study of shamanism and mythology. Powerful group-rituals are for people on the fourth-floor. These require your utmost confidentiality, loyalty and faith. The fifth floor is the training for those very apt practitioners to become a priest or priestess in the Order and to spread the dazzling teachings, powerful blessings, simple sanity and profound beauty all over the world.
We organise introductory weekends several times per year. We are looking for qualified people – trainers and priest(esse)s – to lead the work in every country!

Contact info@advaita-tantra.com for more information.

Glossary

Abhasa	The phenomenal world of the senses
Abhivanagupta	Principal philosopher of Kashmir Saivism (10th century)
Adi Shankar	Great Advaita philosopher of the 9th century
Ahamkara	Ego, I- consciousness
Anugraha	Liberating grace, re-absorbtion, revelation
Anahata chakra	Heart chakra
Avadhna	Vigilant awareness
Bhakti Yoga	Yoga of devotion
Bhoga	Pleasure
Bhogin	Pleasure seeker
Brahma	God as creator
Brahmanandhra	The 1000 petalled Lotus (7th chakra)
Chinnamaste	One of the ten tantric wisdom goddesses
Diksha	Initiation
Divya	Divine ; disciple of the highest qualification
Durga	Tantric goddess in Hinduism
Guru-sisya parampara	Strong current of liberation protected by the masters of the Far East
Hamsa	Mantra used with breathing
Hatha Yoga	Yoga of bodily postures
Himvati	Wife of Shiva born anew as personification of Himalaya's
Iccha shakti	Will in the Absolute to manifest
Ida	Major psychic channel which conducts shakti energy
Ishvara	Lord of the universe
Jivatma	Atman appearing as embodied being
Jnana Yoga	Yoga of knowing, discrimination
Kali	Tantric goddess of beauty and heroism
Kali Yuga	Cosmic era we are living in now in which spiritual level is lowest

Kama	Sensual love
Karma Yoga	The path of selfless action
Kashmir Saivism	Philosophy of Grace; tantric philosophy of Kashmir
Kriya	Spontaneous dynamic activity
Kundalini	The serpent power that can be activated to full awakening
Loka	Plane of existence
Lord Nataraja	Shiva as Lord of the dance
Maharishi	Great seer
Mahavidyas	The great powers of the Mother Goddess (Tara, Kali etc)
Maheshvara	Name of Shiva especially when named together with Brahma and Vishnu
Mala	Limitation, ignorance that hampers the free expression of the spirit
Manas	Mind
Manipura	Third chakra
Mantra	Sacred sounds and magic formulas
Mouna	Inner silence and abstaining from speaking
Nadis	Energy channels in the body
Niscam Seva	Selfless service
Paramashiva	Supreme Reality/Being
Paravak	Transcendental sound as source of creation
Parvati	Wife, devotee and guru of Shiva
Pasu	The ignorant person
Pingala	A major channel for Shakti
Prakriti	Basic substance of the objective world
Pratyabhijna	Recognition of 'I' as divine Self
Prithivi	The earth tattva
Purusha	Pure consciousness, witness
Rajas	The quality of being active – a constituent of Prakriti
Raja Yoga	The path of mind control
Rishi	One who can see intuitively
Sadguru	Spiritual guide of the highest order
Sadhak	An initiate who pactises strong spiritual discipline according to the scriptures or guidelines of guru

Sadhana	Spiritual practice
Shaktipata	Direct transmission of energy from guru to disciple
Samsara	The worldprocess; the process of birth, death, rebirth
Samskaras	The seeds produced by karma
Satchidananda	Truth, consciousness, bliss
Sattva guna	The quality of clarity and purity
Shakti	The dynamic aspect of Shiva
Shiva	The absolute, the transcendent divine principle
Siddhis	Psychic powers
Spanda	Creative pulsation of Absolute Consciousness
Sushumna	The primary, final and very difficult to pierce channel for kundalini
Swadhisthana chakra	2nd Chakra
Tamas	The quality of laziness and inertia
Tara	Goddess of compassion
Tattvas	Grades of existence
Tripura	Goddess of wisdom
Uma	A form of the wife of Shiva
Vaisnava	A worshipper of some aspect of Vishnu
Vamacara	Left handed path in Tantra
Vira	Noble person, hero
Viracara	The path of the hero

Recommended literature

Eric Baret:	Songs of the Ultimate
Coleman Barks:	Naked songs - Lalla
Bhaskar Bhattacharyya:	The Path of the Mystic Lover
Harsha V. Dehejia:	Parvatidarpana
David Frawley:	The Ten Mahavidyas
N.K. Kotru:	Sivastotravali of Utpaladeva
Daniel Ladinsky:	The Gift, poems by Hafiz
Swami Lakshmanjoo:	Vijnana Bhairava
Paul du Marchie:	Philosopher of the great vertigo
Kamalakar Mishra:	Kashmir Saivism
Swami Muktananda:	Play of Consciousness
Mikhail Naimy:	The Book of Mirdad
Daniel Odier:	Desire: The Tantric Path to Awakening
B.N. Pandit:	Specific Principles of Kashmir Saivism
Baird T. Spalding:	Masters of the Far East
Osho:	The Book of Secrets
Dr. Vijay Shankar:	The Illusions of Life
Jaideva Singh:	Siva Sutras
Jaideva Singh:	Spanda Karikas
Jaideva Singh:	Pratyabhijnahrdayam
Jaideva Singh:	Vijnanabhairava
Robert Svaboda:	Aghora (I, II en III)
Pandit Rajmani Tigunait:	Tantra Unveiled
Dr. S.S. Toshkhani:	Lal Ded

BOOKS OF RELATED INTEREST FROM NAB

MOVEMENTS WITH THE COSMIC DANCER

On Pilgrimage to Kailash Manasarovar

—Lakshmi Bandlamudi

On the world stage, each individual self is an actor/dancer. On the Cosmic Plane, Shiva alone is the great Dancer in Great Time choreographing various scenes in the Great Universe. This is the journey of an ordinary pilgrim to an extraordinary place on the Earth. A journey woven with a personal tale of a daughter's search for her lost father. A tale of a soul longing to dance with the Movements of the Cosmic Dancer.

ISBN: 81-7822-280-9

KAILASH MANSAROVAR

Diary of a Pilgrim

—Nilesh D. Nathwani

This profusely illustrated travelogue is a tale about fancies and fears, adventures and aspirations, expectations and disillusions, escapes and retreats experienced by a team of adventurous pilgrims. This is a story of an unforgettable odyssey to the holy Mount Kailash and the sacred Mansarovar describing mysteries connected with the land capturing the intangible air of faith and pilgrimage. This travelogue takes us on a journey to the wild, seldom travelled northern route visiting the remote cities, towns and monasteries of mysterious Tibet.

ISBN: 81-7822-054-7

THE ESSENTIAL VEDĀNTA

A New Source Book of Advaita Vedānta

—Eliot Deutsch, Rohit Dalvi

The Essential Vedānta is a comprehensive introduction to the tradition of Advaita Vedānta based upon primary sources and makes possible a study of its classical form. Translations from major Sanskrit writings are included as well as selections from all of the most important representations of this central philosophy of India.

ISBN: 81-7822-265-5

THE PRINCIPAL UPANISHADS

A Poetic Transcreation

—Alan Jacobs

The origins of the Upanishads, sacred writings of Hinduism, predate recorded history. They are thought of by many as perhaps the greatest of all the books in the history of world religions. Since they were revealed to the Rishis of the Vedic civilisation some 5,000 to 10,000 years ago, many have come to regard them as the kernel of the mystical and philosophical truths that are the basis of understanding religion today. Alan Jacobs has used free modern verse to convey the essential meaning and poetry of the original text, omitting Sanskrit words as much as possible and providing a clear, contemporary commentary.

ISBN: 81-7822-238-8

THE HINDU MIND

Fundamentals of Hindu Religion and Philosophy for All Ages

—Bansi Pandit

Hinduism is the oldest surviving religion in the world. The religious and philosophical literature of Hinduism is vast, diverse and covers thousands of years of accumulated spiritual experiences of Hindu Saints and Seers. This book presents the fundamental Hindu religious and philosophical thoughts in a logical and straightforward manner. The purpose being to create a story book for further study of Hinduism.

ISBN: 81-7822-007-5

EXPLORING MEDITATION

Master the Ancient Art of Relaxation and Enlightenment

—Susan G. Shumsky

This spiritual self-help book offers easy, step-by-step procedures to master the ancient arts of meditation and enlightenment. It offers practical techniques to increase love, power, and energy; reduce stress and tension; improve health;reverse aging; and bring well-being, and peace of mind to everyday life. This book demystifies abstract concepts and provides a road map to the inner life, leading beginners safely through the maze of the spiritual path, pointing out signposts and pitfalls along the way.

ISBN: 81-7822-296-5